An Anthology of Radical Thoughts & Empowering Perspectives

MARCUS M MOTTLEY PH.D

First Edition
Library of Congress Cataloging-in-Publication Data

ISBN: 1452814171
EAN-13: 9781452814179
LCCN: 2010916899

For my sons… Tijani and Yohance. Your future is in your hands… Rise to the occasion! Be gentle! Be passionate and compassionate! Be creative! And… Live spiritually!

For the Children of Antigua and Barbuda…
The future of our country is in your hands…

- Treat it gently!
- Protect it passionately!
- Develop it creatively and intelligently!
- Protect the land!
- Keep the land!
- Own the land!

TABLE OF CONTENTS

PREFACE

The articles and poems in this book were written over a period of 25 years. They represent my thoughts, ideas, ideals and deep feelings on a variety of topics.

You the reader can decide whether or not you agree with the various positions that I take. I hope what comes across to you is my passion, strong sense of justice (or injustice) and deep yearnings.

In the early period, 1982 to 1984, I wrote tens of articles which were published in various Antiguan newspapers, particularly the Worker's Voice. I can only find a few of those articles – those which you find between these covers. These articles were mostly stowed away by my mother to whom I am very grateful for her vision. "Sometime in the future, you may need to read these again!" Back then, I didn't agree... Now here we are... and you, I hope, will be similarly grateful for her foresight. Of course, these articles survived a couple of hurricanes, several floods and at least two major moves!

With respect to my mother's foresight and vision, I am compelled to share this with you. When I was around twelve years old, my mother forced me to take typing and shorthand lessons. I say 'forced' because I was very resistant. Typing and shorthand were for girls who wanted to become secretaries. And since, I had no intention of becoming a secretary... well... you understand my reasoning.

My mother was adamant. So, several times per week, I went to typing lessons at Ms. Francis Typing school in lower gambles (behind Princess Margaret Secondary School). I didn't do well with the shorthand lessons… and soon dropped out of those classes. But typing? I absolutely loved it. Pretty soon, I was typing 70, 80, 90+ words per minute. According to my recollection… I hit the century mark on a few occasions.

My mother even sacrificed and bought a typewriter for me so that I could practice at home.

That typewriter and my mother's insistence on me taking typing lessons are very much related to my writing. I found it easy to type my own articles and submit them to editors. I became my own secretary. And when I started college, it was easy to type all those long papers, reports, studies, and even my dissertation.

I can truly say that my journey of writing and typing essays and poems was made much easier because of my mother's insistence that I learn to type.

To my 96 year old Mom, I say – "Thank you."

I am on another journey. The journey of tracking down other articles from that early period and hope to present them in the forthcoming follow-up to this book: A Second Helping of Radical Thoughts & Empowering Perspectives.

I have been asked why I stopped the flow of articles after 1984. The answer is that I left Antigua in August of that year and came to Washington, DC to pursue higher education… a lifelong dream. That educational odyssey turned out to be a decade long. In between those years, I penned many articles – many as school/course assignments and a few others as contributions to a few Caribbean newspapers in the Washington, DC area. I have recently found some of those articles and they will appear in the sequel to this book.

Thank you for purchasing this book. I hope you find it at least stimulating and thought provoking.

Marcus M. Mottley, Ph.D.
December 2010

That 'Shhhht' Cart

Published in the Antigua Worker's Voice, 1982

Captained by a veteran from far rural west;
The cart does its tours while most people have their nightly rest;
This is a real land cruiser – a relic from antiquity...
A horrible menace to the health of any community.
That cart not seen, not heard, but its passage unmistakable... awfully smelly!

Watchmen usually comfortable at their stations – abhor its passing...
No place to run, no place to hide,
Only a dirty handkerchief as sweet perfume, to mask their loathing.
Quick... duck into the alley... Uncle Tom and the crew must be coming!
Not seen, not heard – but its passage unmistakable – sickening!

The movie goers, the disco lovers, people coming from night mass,
Even for those who many hours after – by the corners they walk past,
They scamper and run for cover – gasping, choking, disgusted, nauseating.
Drivers at the taxi stand, sit in their cars,
With windows closed tightly – to no avail even if they are afar...
The cruiser – not seen, not heard, but its passage unmistakable – revolting!

Car tires and fenders, and some shoe soles (bare feet too),
Render tangible evidence, that the carts' passage leaves our
roads tainted… and painted.
Of course that's not enough pollution,
So the CBH workers add quicklime to the spilled foul
emulsion.
Not heard, but now the evidence seen – absolutely disgusting…

And those in authority… prattle about fig skins and sweetie
paper.
And that our citizens "will be fined if they litter"
"Who" I ask, "will take responsibility for the horror spilt in our
roads and gutters by those infamous 'shhhht' carts - nightly?"
Have you covered your eyes to this ominous custom…
a possible scourge like the Black Death that wiped out
millions?
Not seen, not heard by our 'modern day' leaders and
politicians.

To those who live in other areas,
In your condominiums, executive houses and your palaces,
You who feel far removed from this problem -
To what do you credit your insulation?
We breathe the same air, walk the same streets,
We rub shoulders at parties, at work, at schools, on the street
corners.
Are you immune to the spread of diseases?
Not heard, maybe not seen, but definitely affected
(or is it infected?)

You who have been quiet too long,
It will be forever – before we can right this wrong,
Be quiet, you say, it will run the tourists,
While our children suffer sicknesses without obvious origin -
Flu – stampede, gastro-enteritis – round worms, skin problems –
almost cureless diseases!

Ask those clinic nurses!

My heart goes out to the woman who slipped on Popeshead
Street.
It was a wet day and the white-lime had turned gray.
She tried to avoid this horror,
And sprawled half in the road and half in the gutter!
Dirtying her hair, bruising her palms and knee,
My head reels, my stomach churns,
Do you realize we are all in jeopardy?

Each time you pass that white lime -
Remember that you are exposed to a menace undefined.
Each step you take raises little puffs,
And if there is a slight breeze – and you sneeze…
You will know for certain that you have sniffed…
Some deadly – gray, white, fluffy, 'shhhty' snuff!
Careful now, you must not drop anything,
Because you cannot afford to pick it up again…
Not only seen and heard – but now inhaled and touched!
Gross, unhealthy… stuff!

And that 'shhhh' cart…
Let's get rid of it!
Don't treat it like a State secret.
New school buses, new ambulances, and new APUA trucks …
But no new 'ship' carts – WE HOPE!
What we need is a modern system,
So that as you promise… our Nation can progress
Toward Total Health by the Year 2000!

THE BITTER PILL LITTER BILL

Published in the Workers Voice, November, 1982

On Monday last on Radio
I heard that man, "the Big 'O'"
   (or Bigot)
Introducing the Litter Act
He spoke of Wardens, fines, and this and that
And in truth I first felt sad
Then I got mad...
   at the fact
That Government has nothing to support
   This Litter, Bitter Act

Prompted, maybe by his no conscience
Or perchance, by Mayfield's Health Song
Something just had to be thought up -
As usual, since its close to election!?
But definitely, one can see the lack of preparation
In the itchie-ditchie tut-tut prattling of some simpleton
Or is it from a Statesman, proud of his stint at Education...?
Proud of his ability to produce his own pollution -
   salt water confusion?

Ah... but what preparation?
How do you suppose, rubbish from Greenbay will be collected?
An area like Gray's Farm where most street corners are dumps,
Will you build enough bins
For those old boxes, tin cans, old clothes, etc to be discarded in?
Imagine the wardens picking up some old lady
   for dumping stale food and old shoes on the corner

which is the traditional community rubbish heap centre!!!
Where are those BINS (or whatever)?
And do you have the trained manpower?
    (Not those old, retired, tired pensioners)

To do the work and do it right,
Do you have enough carts (to do the work day and night)?
A major complaint in every area
    is that – for weeks no one sees the garbage collector.
There is no proper system – no real infrastructure.
And who most of all does suffer?
The people from Point, Grays Green, Ottos, etc.
The people with the least facilities,
    and the biggest need for assistance in their areas
They don't even have water…
    So everything gets stuck in the gutter!

Is it for the tax – is it for the money you need?
If that's the real reason for this law… then TAKE HEED!
Because when it comes to littering… you are the biggest culprit.
Ask them people on Union Road
Every 'Cart' that passes, sheds half of its load…
    This happens night and day!
And the guests at those hotels down there say
    that they can can't stand the mess
    (including from the 'shhht' cart)
    That gets spilt all over the roadway!

I support any Act for Public wealth
But I can't stand any shim sham – particularly
    when it comes to health
Let's get the priorities right –
    Public health education, trained personnel, proper vehicles,
    Large refuse bins – spread around the whole community
    And a collection system that takes in everybody – and
regularly

and a modern sewage system.
Too long you have turned your backs to this dangerous
problem,
    Quick lime and water is the wrong solution!
Get rid of those leaky "shhht carts'
    or prepare for public indictment!
Forget about that Litter Act – for now.
You still have a litter of problems to work out
    and that's a fact
You don't have the infrastructure to support that Bill,
If you fine anyone for littering,
    remembering that CBH does the most spilling...
How in Heaven's name did you get the 'cart' before the
horse?
Man, don't you know you have to build foundations first?
Take your medicine and swallow that Bitter Pill Litter Bill
Take a walk in Gray's Farm or up Greenbay Hill
What are you going to do?
    Fine the whole community (or lock up the representative)?

It is good when you have nice roads and houses near the street
side,
Then you can place your bin outside,
But its different on a block with 25 to 60 homes,
    With passages, footpaths, muddily honeycombed –
    What then?
Oh, well, I don't expect you to understand,
Not with a stiff necked, pinched nosed,
    Hurry health on paper plan for "by the year 2000"
expression,

But take heed! That Bill makes no sense,
Not in the face of CBH's incompetence
Not in the face of Government's littering,
Not in the face of infrastructure lacking
Not in the face of that nightly spilling

Not in the face of the total lack of Public Education and planning,
Not in the face of your sit down in the office Bill Making…
GET RID OF THAT BITTER PILL LITTER BILL!
   UNTIL…

EDUCATION FOR OUR YOUTH

Published in the Workers' Voice, 1982

What greater or better benefits can we offer the republic than to teach and instruct our youth? (Cicero, Roman Statesman & Orator)

Many adults are concerned about the problems which face our young people today. One major area of concern is education. In order to determine the depth and breadth of this problem, we must ask ourselves a few questions:

1. How many students reach and successfully graduate from the Secondary School Level? What does 'successfully graduate' mean? What are the standards for success?

2. What alternative programs are there for continuing education which may be available for drop-outs from the formal school system? If there are alternative programs, are they sufficient, and what is their focus?

3. Is the general education program effective? How does it properly and realistically prepare students for working and living? Are students prepared for higher education?

One of the greatest problems facing education is the lack of up-to-date statistics. For example, we do not know what our population is, so how can we know how many children are *not* at school? Quite recently, a wooden house was destroyed by fire in the Gray's Farm Community. This happened on a Wednesday at about 10:30 a.m. at which time adults are usually at work and children at school. I was amazed not at the rapid destruction of the house, but at the huge crowd of children of all ages who poured forth into the road from the alleys and homes to gawk and gape at the fire.

In order to begin to look at our educational policy we need demographic information. How many children of school age live in Greenbay, Grays Farm, or Old Road? What are their ages? How many of them are registered in schools? Which schools are they registered in? What is the percentage of drop-outs from the school-system? How does one area of Antigua and Barbuda compare with another (e.g. Villa area vs. English Harbour)? What comparisons can be made on performance per school and per age level?

There are a host of other questions to be answered, but where is the information? Can we develop policy only on whims, fancies, and politics – totally divorced from hard facts?

I once had the opportunity to visit the State College on the day when the entrance examination was in progress. I am quite sure that there were about six hundred hopefuls up there that morning. I am also quite sure that another six hundred did not bother to apply for one reason or another. Believe it or not, I think that these are conservative numbers. The point here is that there is or seems to be an alternative program for drop-outs from the Secondary School system.

But is it enough? Can one small technical college suffice for students from Antigua, Turks & Caicos, Anguilla, Nevis and St. Kitts? Take into consideration also, that this College accepts students from a certain scholastic level. What happens to the many drop-outs who have not reached this level?

Education should prepare the student to function effectively in a world which is growing more and more complicated. It should cover life in the home – comprehending what we hear and see in the media, understanding how home appliances work, effectively communicating with members of our family, on the job understanding and following directives (written or verbal), proper work attitude and important job skills.

It is not for the certification that we need education, but for the ability to fully utilize our potentials in thought, word and skillful deed. It is the tool used to shape and direct, carve and train our young people into the flexible personalities which must guarantee the continued existence of the human kind.

Education at primary and secondary level is the corner stone on which any nation must be built. It cannot be the privilege of a certain few because of their class or position. I have no doubt that we all agree to this. But how many of us actively work to make this a reality?

Children from poor, over-populated areas and those who belong to sub-cultural groups have the same right to a thorough high level education, reading the same books, listening to the same level of teachers as those children of affluent parents. I have heard of officials of the highest office say, "those children are dunce", in referring to children who failed primary school examinations.

As a former teacher who taught at the Greenbay Government School for almost six years, I refute that, and such statements like that. If children are properly taught and given all the necessary opportunities for learning, they will learn… and learn well. It is an undisputed fact that of all the persons with university degrees, very few of them are above average intelligence, and much less of these can ever be considered as brilliant. How many of you successful businessmen and professionals would honestly consider yourselves to have been brilliant or even above average students in your school days? I dare you to lie!!!

Our primary and secondary level education is the feeder road through which our architects, intellectuals, sportsmen, doctors, lawyers, economists and politicians labored on their journey to their highways.

Life is not as simple as it was then. They were sent to school — and they went. Then, teachers, parents and other adults all 'knocked one head' on the topic of discipline. Not so today. Then, if you passed your exams, you knew jobs were there for you. Even the "Seventh Standard Certificate" was a major achievement. As a matter of fact, many of our Senior Civil Servants have no other qualification. It was... and still is something to be proud of.

Today life is more complex and confusing. Children hear and see conflicting sets of values on television. Their patents may practice one set and preach another. Their teachers do not discipline... many do not seem to care... and they have their own personal problems to deal with. Having G.C.E. Certificates do not guarantee any job... and now there is talk of another certificate? These are just a few examples of the confusing complex situations which face our students. Thus many older people make the mistake of comparing children today with their own youth. There is no comparison. It is a different world we now live in.

We must open our eyes to the real situation. We are now living in the Nuclear and Computer age. Though Antigua and Barbuda is classified as under-developed, this should only refer to things like economics. It cannot and should not refer to the way we think and how we plan for our youths. Our educational program should be comparable to any space age program. We should leave no stone unturned in our efforts to give our young people opportunities we did not and could not have.

In the final analysis, if our children are 'dunce' it is because we have made them so!

THE DIGNITY OF THE PERSON

Published in The Workers Voice – November 24th 1982

Modern society today emphasizes the need to develop a strong, pleasant and magnetic personality. So true is this that many people spend a lot of time on the development of their personality, for they realize that their own happiness and success in life will come from such development.

The ideal personality is one which demonstrates qualities of tolerance, humility, cheerfulness, justice, compassion, love blended in a tranquil and disciplined mind and possessing a powerful ability to focus.

As we build and create our personality today, it will act and express itself in the future. We are today what we have made ourselves in the past through our various physical, emotional, spiritual and social experiences.

Modern psychology stresses that we must be assertive rather than timid. We must try to and understand ourselves – realistically. Active and vibrant introspection is prescribed by the ancient advice: "Know thyself." It is only when we really understand ourselves and other people that we shall find the true value of our existence.

In our efforts to create the ideal personality we must try to visualize what to us constitutes this. We will come to realize that it is by passing through many differing kinds of experiences that we will achieve what we ultimately desire.

"Life is a ceaseless conflict of opposites" said Heraclitus. We must live life to the fullest, meeting circumstances head on, neither avoiding decisions nor running from difficulties. We must face events with self reliance and self-discipline. Perhaps the surest sign of real inner-development will be revealed in our ability to remain cool, calm and composed during these difficult times of ideological and geo-political strife, economic hardships and religious conflicts.

It only takes a few minutes to read the obituaries and to check what some of the general causes of sickness, disease and death are: hypertension, heart problems, nerve disorders and mental illness, drug addiction and alcoholism, ulcers, suicides... These and other diseases have roots in the lack of composure – inability to remain calm – doubt, worry and fear.

Thus, composure involves qualities and characteristics such as: tolerance, humility, compassion, understanding, strength, inner confidence, and a magnetic personality. Such will be the description of a Dignified Person.

SOLITUDE

Published in the Workers' Voice December 1, 1982

"Sometimes I just want to go off by myself, away from people, to breathe freely, to be alone. But I am so busy and there's no place to go!"

This statement depicts a problem among young and old alike. People need solitude, freedom from noise, to get away from the pressures of the workplace and even sometimes from the home. Living today places all kinds of demands and stresses on us. We are constantly on the go. There are so many things to do and people to see that we have very little time or ourselves. And too little time is spent hustling to prepare our meals, bathing, dressing and – sleeping.

We need time to assess our general performance, to see if we are still on track with our goals and ambitions and to make the necessary adjustments. We need a 'breather' so that physical, emotional and spiritual energies can be replenished. We need to take stock.

Our ears need freedom form noises which damages both body and mind. Silence is golden. It is also healing. How many times have we listened to the sounds of nature without interruption: the crickets, the breeze blowing through the trees, the rain on the roof, distant laughter?

Solitude gives us the opportunity to isolate ourselves temporarily from outside interferences, to be able to think through ideas, problems and occurrences in order to attain understanding, solutions and guidance.

Much of our life involves serious thoughts. We may not all become profound thinkers. But most of us can learn to think at a deeper level than we ordinarily do. Being alone allows us to think deeply. Education does not necessarily determine depth of thought. But observation, meditation, reflection and active reasoning do — if we give ourselves a chance.

Being alone makes you feel closer to yourself. We are constantly being bombarded with information, ideas, feelings and experiences. We need time to allow these to soak in.

Retired people, who have lots of new time to think, realize that they would have benefitted tremendously had they stopped to think and review issues during their more active years. We should learn from them.

Some people complain that they do not have enough time. A few minutes after dinner... before bedtime... after church — a few minutes to be alone.

Jesus Christ, John the Baptist, Moses, the biblical prophets, the Buddha — all utilized solitude as a technique for introspection and spiritual communication.

You too can do this for your total benefit. When you feel crowded: the children, the noise, the neighbors, the bills, your spouse, your parents, your job — just about everything... Take some time off.

Take a drive in the country. To Shirley's Heights maybe? Sit by the beach or on your gallery, or out in the yard. Take a walk or sit quietly in your bedroom. And – think, reflect, meditate, relax an turn things over in your mind.

Do this regularly and you discover a gold mine – a source of radiant light within yourself.

Live Life to the Fullest

Published in the Workers' Voice December 4, 1982

When we take a close look, we will admit that we are the ones who are preventing ourselves from experiencing a fuller life. Among things, we have allowed certain social restrictions to limit us. Are you shy? Why? Are you afraid what people will say or think of you? Are you worried about being rejected? Do you feel left out?

Do you want to be friendly? Well, why not? Say hello and hold a friendly conversation with the next person you meet and are attracted to. There is something mystical about friendliness, kindness and politeness. Only very strange or sick persons can resist them. And even then, I am sure that deep inside, those same people are responding positively.

If you have an urge to do something, give yourself a chance to try it. Do you want to play an instrument? Play tennis? Write a book or act a play? Learn a foreign language? What about changing your job? Go to an exercise class, start taking dancing lessons or try jogging.

Do something new and different. Look at the people you admire... what makes them different? They have dared to do something that you would like to do... to be the person that you would want to be... that is why you admire them!

Whether you are young, middle aged, or aged, there is something for you. Just look within yourself and determine what would be a worthy challenge. If you are a woman and you want to play cricket, or you are man you would like to play netball… no one is stopping you… Just have a go at it.

Remember you can benefit from the experience of others and avoid the pitfalls they suffered. Read about determined people. For example, read about the Black belt karateka who has no legs or the one armed base ball pitcher. Beethoven, one of the greatest composers of all time, lost his hearing and was unable to outwardly enjoy his own music.

Truly great people have had to suffer defeat, rejection and disappointment. Read some biographies of great men and women, learn about determination, perseverance and the kinds of attitude necessary to keep going.

Have faith in yourself.

Take note of the fact that living a full life does not guarantee constant happiness. Trials and tribulations, pain and suffering… are all inherent in life. Identify any great person… anyone who lived a full life who didn't have to endure – Abraham? Martin Luther? Joe Louis? Marcus Garvey? We can only appreciate joy when we know sadness. Our laughter is sweetest after a few moments of tears.

To live fully, we must have challenge; an opportunity to make choices – both right and wrong – to learn and experience as many things as we can. "The world is a stage and we are all actors on it."

Do not get lost in the audience… but take the stage, not once… not twice… but as often as possible. Perform in as many plays as you can, act in different roles, and live life to fullest!

GREATER PRODUCTIVITY

Published in The Workers Voice, 11th December, 1982

Productivity has been defined as the relationship between the physical, mental output of a person, company or a nation and the input of skills, know how, labor, capital and materials. In simple words it is the relationship between input and output.

When we look at our periodicals, today, we find the headlines reveal high levels of unemployment, sluggish economies, high numbers of High School dropouts, low levels of High School passes, companies declaring bankruptcies, and much more. The roots of some of those problems undoubtedly lie in the sphere of low productivity.

Productivity must be seen from an individual and personal standpoint. When a school is highly rated it means that the individuals in the school produce – the head teacher produces – the class teacher produces – and each student produces. It means that there is high academic performance, good behavior and success in extra-curricular activities. The same production ratio can be used with any institution, company, industry… and even a nation. Productivity then must be taken personally.

Of course there are many factors which affect one's productiveness. Some of these are: educational and cultural background, personal interests, aptitudes and abilities, experiences, age, skill and expertise, financial conditions, physical and material resources, health, family life and the national and international environment.

Of these, educational and cultural backgrounds play the key role. It is during our childhood years at home and at school that we learn valuable qualities such as self discipline, respect and good behavior. It is also at this time that we practice punctuality, effective communication, decision-making, logical reasoning, proper work attitudes towards assignments and learn to adopt high performance habits.

At least, it is at this time that we should learn these things. But the facts belie this situation. Let us examine our schools: the high levels of absenteeism and lateness; the lack of total involvement in actual activities (or the lack of opportunities for involvement); the low levels of discipline; the erosion of traditional standards of behavior; the large amount of dropouts; the low performance level in school and poor achievement at exams; and, the general attitude towards assignments (homework).

Let me hasten to add that at this time I am not blaming anyone. However, if the child does not do his homework and is not motivated to produce in school, what will his work attitude be like as an adult? If at sixteen years of age he has developed a negative outlook or even an indifferent approach to punctuality and attendance, do you think he will be a changed person ten years later?

Although, productivity must be seen from an individual viewpoint this does not relieve our institutions of their responsibilities. Adequate steps must be taken immediately on a national front to motivate the individuals in our society to change their attitudes towards productivity. This must involve a scientific approach to education, career guidance, personal development programs, vocational training and community development projects.

Whatever is done must have a three pronged approach: (1) Home and family; (2) School and community; (3) Jobs or professions. Also of equal importance are styles and methods of teaching and management: incentives for increased production; more opportunities for local and other training seminars for adult groups on topics such as personal development, parenting and self-help projects.

As an individual, are you satisfied with your performance at school? At work? As a husband? As a parent? Are you satisfied that what you are putting in on the job is on par with what you are getting out? Do you think too much is asked of you for the 'too little' reward you are given at month's end? Does this thought affect your attitude and behavior thereby affecting your performance and productiveness?

Only you can really answer these questions. Be honest with yourself; reflect on your skills, know-how, your attitudes and attendance. Make high productivity a personal issue in all spheres of your life. Do everything in your power to improve and progress, and to develop your inputs and outputs.

Remember that "As you sow, so shalt thou reap."

Enjoying Our Island Paradise

Published in The Workers' Voice, December 23rd 1982

Every year thousands of tourists visit and enjoy our little island. For some of them this is a once in a lifetime vacation. They had been planning and saving for this holiday trip for years. Certainly, there must be something here which they find attractive. If we were to eavesdrop a little, we would probably hear them use words such as 'refreshing', 'peaceful', 'beautiful', 'enjoyable', 'tasty', and 'friendly'.

Not only do thousands of tourists come here each year, but many repeat their visits, and some even spend up to three months here. What do they find so irresistible on our fair shores? Do we Antiguans experience similar feelings for our own island?

Would you take a holiday here? I do not mean that you should spend your vacation cooped up in your house. No! Would you stay at a guest house, at a hotel, with a friend in the country, or rent a beach house for a month? Or, if you find these unsuitable, would you take some weekends off and familiarize yourself with your country?

There are many Antiguans who do not know where Brown Bay is, or have never been to Mosquito Cove. Have you been to Bats' Cave, Monk's Hill, Mt. Mc Nish, Seaforth's Bay, Body Pond, Turtle Bay, or Pinching Bay?

Have you been to Barbuda?

Outdoor Values:

As a teacher, I once took a class on a hike through Bendals and up to Mc. Nish Mountain. At the end of the day, we hiked down the other side through Christian Valley and back to town. The path up to Mc Nish was somewhat tiring. But it was worth the feeling of exhilaration, the cool breezes and the uninterrupted view which we commandeered from on top.

Needless to say, I have been back there many times. On that same trip, an old man from Old Road Village, who was tending his coal kiln, directed us to a clear, cold water stream. A stream on top of the mountain! I have never tasted anything as refreshing.

I spend a lot of my spare time walking, driving or doing something somewhere back in the country. It is always a pleasure. The air is fresh, healthy and full of vitality.

If you like fishing, try some of these dams: Potworks, Breaknocks or Dunnings. You may be lucky to catch a crawfish at Creekside (like I did). On the other hand, you can try rock fishing at the Narrows, Fort Berkely or Devil's Bridge. The strong hearted can attempt some fishing trips down the south side of Shirley's Heights. I have been on countless fishing tips, some at sea, but most on solid ground, and the memories of these are still with me.

The Beach:

It is positively enlightening to see the many Antiguans at Fort James and Halcyon beaches early in the mornings and on Sundays. But how many more are missing out on regularly enjoying our beaches? How many reserve this pleasure for Labour Day, Whit Monday or Easter Monday? And even then, some only look at the water while others bathe on the sand.

Many foreigners express great surprise at the fact that few Antiguans can swim well. An hour at the beach can well take the place of some tranquilizer prescribed by your doctor. Swimming, floating or even lying on the sand watching the rippling waves can be physically, mentally and spiritually healing.

It is true that very few of us can afford a room in one of our luxury hotels, or sit down to a lobster dinner in one of our fabulous restaurants. But all of us can enjoy our climate, our food and our beaches. As a matter of fact, many of us do make an effort to enjoy these things. But there are too many people who either are not interested, or are too busy with work or home life to give 'enjoying our island paradise' a second thought. I think that it is the job of the enlightened among us to change this situation.

Years ago, when a club wanted to have a social function or raise money – they organized excursions. Hikes were popular and so were picnics. Picnics are still popular, but only a few beaches like Long Bay, Deep Bay, Fry's Bay or Runaway are frequented. Clubs, community groups and schools when considering walk-a-thons, picnics and hikes must plan outings to new places so that the whole exercise will be novel, educational and exciting.

I have taken foreign groups on roundtrip tours which ended up as an education for the Antiguans on the trip too! A friend told me recently that he was ashamed of the fact that he is one of those Antiguans who do not know Antigua well. There are many places he has never even heard of, and countless others he has not seen - even villages!

Can you imagine that? Are you in the same position? His excuses are that he never had the opportunity when he was younger and he does not have the time now. My advice to him and to those of you who are like him is to make the time.

Transportation to most places is not a problem. Hike it or catch a bus to the nearest village. Convince a friend who owns a car to go along with you. Motivate your class, youth and community group or even your co-workers to have these kinds of outdoor activities.

In conclusion, I advise everyone to make an effort to become a knowledgeable all-rounder on: the history, culture and the geography of our Island Paradise.

To the Old:
If you had been to all those places when you were young – go to them now and re-live the memories of your youth.

To the Young:
It is your right to know your country. Demand it!

To Those in-Between:
Do not allow the young to embarrass you and the old to deride you – replace the shame that you are feeling with a feeling of confidence and knowledge, and during this metamorphosis, experience the exhilarating thrill of living in Antigua – the Gem of the Caribbean.

A NEW LEAF – MAKE A RESOLUTION

Published in The Workers Voice, January 5ᵗʰ, 1983

Day to day, as we progress from birth to death, each of us is creating a story of life unlike all other persons. We live an episode each day and though it be a tragedy, an adventure, a farce or a comedy, it is our experience of life.

In many ways, each new day is the same for everyone. It is a blank page for each on which to write his or her story. Whether prince or pauper, healthy or sick, young or old, the new day is ours to create as we will. Reject all negative and limiting thoughts, forget about whatever advantages others had over us yesterday. That was yesterday. Today, they have the same blank slate as we. What shall we do today? We shall take steps to fill the page with a creative, positive and harmonious episode.

The first step in this endeavour is to control and order our thinking. Many of yesterday's failures were self created by our own negative thinking. The unhappy consequences of our anxieties, fears, hatreds, jealousies, doubts and vexations must be replaced by disciplined, positive thoughts. Decide that today you are going to make positive contributions to the episode. Your episode! Remember, whether positive or negative, something will be written and recorded today.

The second step is to utilize the law of attraction. We attract to ourselves that which we mentally create about us. Attraction is a basic and inviolable law of nature. We will attract whatever dominates our thinking. If we think negatively then our lives will be filled with failures and hard times.

The third step is to produce what we create in our minds. Take a lesson from the book of nature: The hard working and or tiresome busy little bee; the spider continuously spinning its web; or, the beaver who is always building its dam. To grow and attain the goals we have set for ourselves we have to work at it... constantly... by leaving little or no time for cancerous doubts and fears!

The fourth and final step is decision. Decide to change. Decide to accept responsible for things you do and the events in your life. Decide to ignore and eliminate the failures and limitations of the past. Decide that today and tomorrow will be better because we will make it better.

This is the time when most people reflect on the past year and make resolutions for the new year. Remember that last year was a chapter in your life... a long chapter of 365 pages! On reflection, the contents may have been less than satisfactory to us. Do not be ashamed of them. You have lived and experience. Use them as lessons, a guide to the future and pitfalls to avoid. They are finished and unchangeable. Do not regret.

The future is before us unmade and the pages are blank. Resolve to paint pictures of success and harmony. Resolve to write stories of progress, good fortune and accomplishment. Resolve to be both the Captain and Navigator of your ship so that whether the waters are calm or stormy you will be in effective control.

DISCIPLINE

Published in The Workers' Voice, January 1983

Recently, I started playing softball cricket at the PMS play field. One afternoon after batting quite well, I was run out by my partner. (At least this is my side of the story.) In any case, I was engulfed by a wave of frustration and anger. I felt like throwing my bat out of the field! Eventually, I was brought back down to earth by other players who counseled: "Take it easy." "That's the game." "Ah so e go sometime!" These and other comments gradually smoothed out the ruffles.

On reflection, I realized that the incident was a lesson in DISCIPLINE. I realized that when our personal control has been dented and torn, others can help to repair and strengthen it. It also brought out the fact that we can and should share the responsibility for each others actions.

We can also utilize this approach in all our national and regional activities.

For this, we need vision, clear definitions of goals, and the steadfastness to pursue them in joint efforts. All group work requires goodwill, faith, honesty and intelligence. But to work in concert requires the kind of character that can only be molded and held together by DISCIPLINE.

What changes do we have of ever attaining discipline on a national and regional level? The chances seem very slim. According to social psychologists, historians and even our grandparents, there has been a significant breakdown of discipline throughout the whole community. Any teacher can tell you nowadays, that, by and large, discipline in schools is only a concept... not a reality.

There is ample testimony to support the fact that drug abuse and alcoholism is on the increase in all levels of the society. There is also evidence of indiscipline everywhere: from supermarket pilferage by shoppers to grand theft, fraud and embezzlement by people in responsible positions.

There is also evidence of twisted truths, barefaced lies, cover ups and corruption among our political leaders. In this hemisphere, there are also countless intrigues, plots, coup and counter coups for the sake of political power under the guise of ideological theories – all at the expense of many human lives. And then there is active competition between some (all?) of our churches for larger congregations (larger purses?).

What our society has lost, temporarily we hope, is a sense of individual and public responsibility, the recognition of our duties, and the discipline to carry them out. We all are guilty of indiscipline at some level or the other. We may start something new, maybe a series of exercises, but give up if success does not come easily. We may neglect our group duties or find fault, get annoyed and aggravated at others who do not do things our way.

But there is no need to list national, individual or group weaknesses as examples of the loss of discipline. Self examination will reveal them. Our own and the world's problems are not cured by finding fault with others or even with ourselves. Let us instead recognize our duties. Let us get to work and stick with it.

Work is discipline... sticking to it, utilizing stamina is the essence of discipline. Pitching in and helping to bear the weight of others when they falter is also discipline. But most of all, properly preparing and training ourselves so that we are equal to the assigned and self imposed duties is also discipline. All thorough training is harsh but the fruits are sweet. The fully trained athlete, technician and scientist enjoy their own performance although they must continue to exercise discipline through care and concentration on every detail.

Let us all accept the cross of discipline through which we hope to achieve our regional, national and personal goals. Remember though, that this must begin within. Make plans and follow through with them to the sweet end.

Nationally, we must bring discipline into schools and right back into the class rooms. This is the training camp over which we have national control. If changes are to come on any level it must start there. Students must see themselves as individuals set in the framework of a class and school team, a community team and as members of our National team.

"EACH endeavouring, ALL achieving."
"Never failing, ALL enduring".
"Sparing NOTHING, Giving ALL."
These can only be made manifest starting with high levels of individual DISCIPLINE.

THE MANAGER'S CONFLICT OF NEEDS

Published 1983

A manager's world involves the fulfillment of personal
and social needs. Success in meeting these needs results
in satisfaction and happiness at life. Having achieved this
harmony, one feels a sense of bliss, of fulfillment, of being
on top of the world. In truth, this is what Abraham Maslow
refers to as "The state of self-actualization or self-fulfillment."
However very few managers ever reach this state of being. And
for those who do, it has come after passing through the perilous
arena of the conflict of needs which occurs when an individual
is motivated by two or more needs and the satisfaction of one
causes the denial of the other.

Managers, like the rest of us have physiological and social
needs. Hunger, thirst, need for air, temperature control, pain
avoidance, good healthy, sex, activity and stimulation make
up some of our physiological needs. Most of these are usually
well taken care of. However, good health and physical activities
(exercise) sometimes get left behind because of the pressure of
fulfilling certain social and psychological needs.

The number of social/psychological needs is vast. They include
money, status, belonging, acceptance by others, friendship and
love. In order to satisfy these safety, security and status needs,
a manager works long hours, misses important meals, develops
bad habits such as cigarette smoking and builds up inner
tension. In trying to satisfy some of his psychological needs his
physiological needs suffer. In many cases this can be physically
expensive, sometimes fatally so.

There are also other social needs such as friendship and love, companionship and privacy. In order to satisfy these, a manager gets married and for some time, the novelty of home life refreshes and rejuvenates him/her. But, sooner rather than later, the achievement bug gets him/her along with new financial pressures. A new quota of long nights, late meals, unsatisfied and estranged family members develops.

Sometimes, the situation can be altruistic in his or her mind, since all of this effort is usually for the benefit of the family. The manager also pays a high cost for this behavior with health problems. This itself can cause psychological problems. Indeed, it shows itself in smoking, alcoholism, neurotic behavior and even psychotic behavior in rare cases.

The expectations of society also adds fuel to the conflicts that managers experience. People of a 'certain' social standing or status are usually expected to live up to certain norms of behavior such as maintaining a moral public profile, living in a high status residential community, or owning the latest, most expensive car. These are 'musts' even though the family is up to its ears in debt. This status also involves being members in certain clubs: e.g. Lions and Rotary.

These expectations have a profound effect on the individual because these are his/her expectations also. To act contrary to them may cause inner conflicts. To ignore them may lead one to feel that doors will be closed, powerful associates will be missed, and success, achievement, influence and power will fly out through the window.

To live up to these expectations means that personal hobbies, and close personal relationships suffer. The little things which make life most interesting and rewarding suffer the most: playing with the kids, sitting in the garden with one's spouse, visiting parents and grandparents, going for a drive in the countryside, going to the drive-in cinema, reading a book by that favorite author, or sitting and listening to the latest music album. For our health and wellbeing these little things are among our most important strategies to satisfy some of our needs. To deny them their place in life is to turn our back on life itself.

There are other needs which are of great importance to the manager. These can be termed self-esteem and ego needs. They include the desire for respect, strength mastery, competence and confidence. The individual's feelings about himself depend to a large measure on how he believes other people, especially people important to him, see or esteem him. Issues such as his level of dominance and importance in his field, and the levels of public recognition, dignity and appreciation are most important. Thus, the manager is motivated to strive for these factors of public esteem at all costs.

The conflicts, inner and outer, develop, in some cases, to suicidal proportions. This is the case in Japan where there are hundreds of cases each year of managers who commit suicide. In many instances, there is the encroaching of career life on home life… a factor that many managers have never learned to deal with. Anxiety and guilt, frustration and stress cause further erosion in these individuals' lives. Such anxiety is related to doubt and fear.

Thus, one more negative and conflicting feeling develops in direct contrast to the self-confidence which is being strived for. These situations are certainly stressful and can result in frustration over personal limitations, family problems and other negative situations created by personal ambition, and societal pressures and expectations. It is no wonder that each year a small, but statistically significant number of these executives decide that suicide is the most attractive alternative.

The physical side effects of this pepperpot of conflicts are dangerous, crippling and sometimes quite fatal. Hypertension, gastric ulcers, heart disease, nervous disorders are the direct result of tension and stress. Alcoholism and cigarette smoking claim a high percentage of victims from the world of managers through cancer and other diseases.

Imagine for a moment, an individual's inner agony and conflict when he knows that his health is deteriorating and, for example, his lungs are becoming diseased because of his cigarette smoking. And yet, he feels powerless to stop his fingers from reaching for the pack out of his pocket to get the next cigarette. And, during a particularly stressful day, he might smoke two to three packs.

Role conflict also militates against the happiness of a manager. For example, a business woman may be torn between the demands placed on her as a woman to be passive and dependent, and the demands placed on her as a business person to be independent, assertive – or even aggressive, confident and competitive. Imagine a sales executive's organizational role may conflict with his role as a husband and father due to his busy travel schedule.

The conflicts managers face must be resolved in order for the individual to function effectively in all spheres of life. Compromise, which some understand and use effectively at meetings and in business deals, must also enter into the personal arena. The motivating factors must be faced and the priorities set down.

Which things are important? Is my job killing me slowly? Am I happy to give my life to power, status and influence? Or, is peace, time with loved ones and moments of joy with nature important also?

The answers need not spell out the fact that one thing takes precedent over another. Solutions can be worked out where one aspect harmonizes with another. Here is a chance for creativity, for a rethinking and re-structuring of one's life. It is an opportunity for personal development and successful self-management.

Indeed, in attempting to resolve these conflicts, managers would be satisfying the highest level of needs as identified by Abraham Maslow and Douglas McGregor – that of self-fulfillment or self-actualization. This refers to the process of making maximum use of abilities, of developing talents and potential, and of being the sort of person one deeply aspires to be. Self-actualization occurs when one reaches for the highest form of internally driven satisfaction rather than settling for superficial social acknowledgements.

Along with these levels of personal development come self-understanding, continuous self-improvement, and a deepening and broadening capacity to enjoy life in all of its forms. With this type of attitude one sheds the narrowness and single minded selfishness of superficial personal career goals. He or she is then able to see life on a whole and is then better able to deal with any new conflicts that arise.

Self-fulfillment can resolve the manager's conflicts of needs. First must come an awareness of the existing conflicts. Secondly, he or she must determine what the important things are. Having reached this far, the individual must begin to plan and execute their plan so that he or she can manage all aspects of their life effectively.

WHAT IS MISSING?

Published in The Workers' Voice, January 12, 1983

The most familiar words and phrases we hear in the news these days are recession, nuclear wars, global destruction, industrial unrest, border battles, refugees, coup d'etats, famines and family planning. Some of these are also among the most ominous words in any language. The picture may be foreboding but it aptly describes what is actually transpiring on our planet. If we are as concerned as we should be, we must turn our minds to these questions: Why? Is something missing? If so, what?

Experts of various disciplines agree that something is lacking. But they differ on what that something is. Marxists feel that it is the non-acceptance of the communist creed (or its watered down version – socialism) that will lead mankind to global destruction. Christians feel that the world will come to an end because many people have not accepted some their particular teaching or doctrine. Exponents of democracy, capitalism and imperialism believe that the communists are responsible for causing social and political unrest and strife world wide.

Sociologists and psychologists assume that the root of all these problems lie in the breakdown of the traditional rules of behavior and attitude in the home, at school and in the community. Some economists feel that some substance like oil or gold or some form of cheaply harnessed energy is missing. Scientists are exploring the oceans for food and metals, and searching the universe for an alternate planet to Earth.

It cannot be denied that the opinions of all these experts might have some merit. However, let us take a closer look at the situation. Mankind can live in peace and harmony IF the leaders of the world would put aside ideological differences and allow reason to prevail in the common interest of all humanity.

Religion would be much more meaningful, helpful and play a greater role IF churches and religious groups would put aside differences in doctrine and dogma, and preach unity under one God. What difference does it make whether one is a Hindu, Moslem, Jew, Christian, or Buddhist? They all claim to worship the same God!

There is enough food worldwide IF countries were to change their hoarding policies and distribute food on an equitable and humanitarian basis. It would be better IF developed economies were to encourage and help to build less developed ones instead of competing and stifling their growth. There would be less industrial unrest and more employment IF governments were to concentrate on stable home-grown industries like agriculture.

Of course, these are all very big 'Ifs' and the pessimists claim that the present trend will continue because goodwill is lacking. They also have Revelations and prophets of doom like Nostradamus in their camp.

But, "is there not balm...?" Isn't there any answer? Isn't there some guide who will point the way?

The problem is that there may be and may have been several guides... but nobody is really following them. (Do not place all the blame on the flock because the shepherds are in disarray.)

Our political and religious leaders must share much of the blame for the situation in which we find ourselves. For personal power and other selfish ends they have refused to reason with one another, and have adapted cosmetic solutions to entrenched problems. They have been unable to overcome ideological fanaticism and fractional ambitions.

We the flock have been caught in the middle, used and abused as tools and weapons against each other, even against our own families, martyrs for another's cause! We have been crushed between the Arabs and the Jews, the Shah and the Ayutallah, the Bear and the Eagle. We have been abused by the multinational corporations and made emotionally dependent on their useless creations. We have been used even by our own and quite regularly too.

What then can we do? What is lacking? I have no answer for you.

My answer is my own. But, I can share it with you. However, you must develop your own.

Everyone must develop himself/herself from within and come to grips with problems from a personal standpoint. Develop your leadership potential and play a more leading role in your own affairs. Part of the answer, at least, lies in Positive Personal Development.

MOMENTUM

Published in the Antigua Workers' Voice, February 1983

At dawn, cocks crowing
Farmers, their donkeys protesting,
On the way to their grounds for weeding and reaping,
    or their early morning milking...
People at the stand pipe, everywhere water flowing,
    in their homes pots and pans jingling
      the smell of coals burning, or the stove lightly glowing.
Old women at the side of streets, bending with their brooms
    and rakes cleaning and sweeping,
    hustling, to avoid the expected solar heating.

Young athletes in the pasture, on the roads,
    in the gyms, running and exercising.
Hucksters... their trays filled with oranges, bananas,
    mangoes and sugar apples – waiting.
The church bell rings – inviting
Most people awake – only a few still dreaming...
Wake up – you few, it's morning!

The streets now filled with people, hustling lest they
    be left behind, running
    to the bus stop, waiting
    on the corner, or standing
    near their gap.
Some with one eye on the vendors tray,
    the other on the road way.
Nurses, masons, tradesmen, carpenters,
Women in crisp white dresses or pretty skirts and
    fluffy blouses – all hotel workers.

The buses, from the country – loaded beyond capacity
    and on the way back – empty.

Watchmen, fresh from an illegal night's rest,
    Plodding home with stick in the right hand
    and torch in the left.
Weary – not from work – but from age,
    the toll of the bottle added to their years.
Now all around, the sound of Big Ben
    followed by the news
    local, regional, international facts and views,
    Listened by everyone, in their cars, at home, in the bus
    Some received with cheers, others with disgust.

In the streets, overall, hard hats and boots,
Now replaced by shirt-jacks, uniforms and books.
Police carrying out their traffic functions
    at pedestrian crossings and major junctions…
Cars, trucks, bikes, different vehicles
    carrying clerks, teachers and workers in government
Hustling, bustling happily moving towards – gainful
employment.
In the air – an attitude of expectation and of preparation
    making meaningful contribution to the success of the
    nation.

All in all the noise increasing
Horns blowing, people calling – arguing shouting
    no time for gossiping
Men – hammering, brick laying, road building,
    constructing…
In factories, trained workers refurbishing, assemblying
    fabricating – creatively designing – building
Mechanics, electricians and even musicians practicing
Clerks auditing, typing, reporting
    While salesmen persuading.

On the beaches – tourists swarming
　　sunbathing, swimming,
　　enjoying the sunshine, the sea, the spirit of our
Caribbean island
　　they contemplate returning.
On corners, no begging, no limers – no stealing
Out in the fields,
Farmers – backs almost breaking – weeding, sweating
　　tractors ploughing –
　　the smell of freshly turned earth – refreshing
　　crops green – fruits ripening
　　cows, donkeys, sheep – even a dog under a tree...
　　watching...

"Wake Up!"
"It's eight in the morning and you are still in bed sleeping!"
"What happened?"
"Were you dreaming?"
"You certainly were laughing, humming, twisting and even
turning...
　　even smiling."
"You were dreaming, I am certain..." My mom said...
"You were dreaming!!"
I had been dreaming
And how real it had seemed...
"A community – on the move – growing"

But,
I awoke to silence – almost deafening.
No voices, no hammering, no horns blowing.
However, there was some vague silent mutterings,
A few people – slowly treading, loitering, lingering...
The lucky – going and not going.

No work... no play – nothing
　　But politicians all...

Talking – walking around visiting emptily promising –
    encouraging voting
And people not learning
    but hopefully responding – wishful thinking!
And parsons in their pulpit preaching
    without vision and meaning… just rehashing!
In schools – teachers – in staffrooms gossiping
    reading Mills & Boon, sleeping
    at their desks – daydreaming
No hope – no future, no – Nothing.

In the communities
    The gutters – water not moving
    the housing – a problem, no efforts toward solving
    yes… more roads, but more holes, just mere roads
    They need fixing!
Unemployment – the correct figure is appalling.
Education – improper planning.
And the night soil – makes your stomach churn
    and your system boil,
    spilt in the roads and covered with white lime
    this should be considered a public crime
    Yet, everyone afraid to mention
    Closing their minds to this problem-
    though it needs immediate attention.

No wonder we are plagued
    By the Bionic and Stampede
    dysentery and round worms
    and all other germs;
And this a country – supported by a tourist economy?

The list is endless,
    and there is not enough space.
But,
    Things to be said – must be said

Less they clutter the mind
And fill the soul with blame and disgrace.

But,
What is the alternative?
It seems we are forced to live
with what we now have...
the best of the worst this nation has to give!

CAREER GUIDANCE IN OUR SCHOOLS

Published in The Workers' Voice, February 12, 1983

It is an indisputable fact that a large amount of students 'leaving' school today find themselves in a kind of limbo. This is evidenced by the fact that there are a host of unemployed, under-employed and unemployable youths in communities throughout Antigua and Barbuda. There is and will always be official denial as to the amount of such persons. Irrespective of this official denial, you and I personally know of individual youths, families and even communities that face this predicament.

Many of those who I speak of either dropped out of school at the Post Primary stage or at the pre-G.C.E stage. Some students dropped out because there was little hope of them ever passing the traditional Post Primary Exam and then moving on. Others never quite reached that stage. They got stuck in the 'quick sand' at Senior 2B or 'tripped and fell' into the 'bottomless pit' of Senior 3B.

On the other hand, there are those who reached our Secondary schools. One example, which really demonstrates a common occurrence, will serve my various points well. Sandra (not her real name) passed all the subjects of the Post Primary Exam and entered the Secondary School. At that time, she had two years left until she had to take her G.C.E. exam. She was introduced to new subjects like Chemistry and French.

Classes took on a vastly different perspective – being more lecture oriented than the close, individual approach to which she was accustomed at her Junior Secondary School. She was slow in adapting, and the next year, she, along with most of the other students who had passed the Post Primary Exam, were jammed into the business section.

No thought was given to the problems, hopes and ambitions of the student. No thought was given to the questions: "Are we doing the right thing for these students? Is this academic program (where you have Post Primary students join a secondary school in the middle of the school program - two years away from one of the most important examination milestones in their life)? Do students from Post Primary schools have special needs? Is pushing these students into the 'Commercial' program really the only answer? Does Antigua have too many young people 'half learning' Commercial subjects? Are there jobs out there for them?

Do not take my word for it! Do a personal survey on the fate of the Post Primary student who enters the Secondary School system!

Indeed, this is only one of the problems our educational system faces. We must not cast blame unnecessarily either. Criticism must be positive and must be taken positively. However, if we have problems, we must look at solutions.

In determining educational policy we must look at a number of things, some of which are:

1. The individual needs of our youths must be fully examined.

2. The overall goals and plans of our nation must be taken into account when we develop educational policy goals.

3. The national and world economic situation must be examined and considered.

4. The current job market must be examined as well as the near and far future.

5. The population and the social needs of our communities must be considered.

Having looked at these and other considerations, we must develop our educational policy and let it be known to everyone. This cannot be treated like a top secret, but must be known and conscientized by the Nation. It must become common knowledge.

Work is the most import, most meaningful and most essential activity in which everyone on Earth participates or aspires to participate in. One's career or job determines his way of life, health and happiness and self value. It determines how a person interacts with the rest of society. Is he bitter or is he satisfied? Can he afford to get married? Can he take care of the family adequately? Can the family afford to purchase school books?

If, then, our careers, jobs or work affect the foundations of our daily life and are of such prominence and importance to us, shouldn't we give it the same amount of emphasis in our school program? Our curriculum must not only include things like History, Religious Knowledge, English Literature and French, but must include practical subjects which everybody faces daily.

These may include basic accounts, effective communication (oral and written), personal development, problem solving techniques, goal setting and specific aspects of the work world. These are but some of the areas which could be covered in a comprehensive Career Guidance Program.

As adults, we must look at the problems we have, and have had in selecting a career, getting a job and keeping it. We must realize that irrespective of what we hear officially, meaningful employment is not on the increase. (The amount of students coming out of schools is on the increase.) Trainee 'jobs' may be on the increase, but these are only stop-a-gaps which leave participants feeling like hangers-on and misfits. If the training was planned, monitored, evaluated and set in a timeframe we could take another close look at it.

But after that training... then what?

We need a comprehensive Career Guidance Program which meaningfully reflects public policy towards our economic development, other national plans, our awarding of work permits, and the development of our financial institutions, which should together openly encourage not only employment... but self-employment.

"We commit ourselves to building a true Nation" ... " 'Gainst fear, hate and poverty."

A New Code of Morals - *Part 1*

Published in The Workers' Voice – March 12, 1983

Morality has not always been the subject of much discussion in any so-called civilized society.

Generally, our past has given us a vast heritage of moral concepts, beliefs and even superstitions upon which the moral concept of our society is built. These constitute codes of conduct which are accepted by most people. For example: In a 'civilized' society it is generally agreed that one should not steal, kill or rape. The wrongdoer has always been in the minority and usually punished by society – though such punishment has always been consistently applied. Sometimes society has actually protected the violator depending upon the social status of the individual offender.

Today, there are obvious signs that certain parts of society are no longer willing to comply with the existing codes without resistance, arguments or even more tangible and vigorous actions. These people realize that the society in which we are born is the furthest thing from being perfect: war, poverty, starvation, inequality, famines, slavery, political domination, religious hypocrisy, crime, social decadence, illness… and these are drawn from an ever increasing list!

Religious priests are fighting as guerillas; teachers in all our larger universities are encouraging rebellion, teaching and preaching subversion; political leaders encourage social strive and diversion either to remain in power or to usurp power; companies and industrial barons reap harvest by doing irreparable damage - to our ecological health with their smut and industrial waste – and to our economy with their high prices (whatever the market will bear mentality)!

Additionally, both individuals and institutions are providing information and examples of the wrong kind... the immoral kind. Are our leaders – religious, social and political displaying the kinds of morals that we can use ourselves?   No!

But, then what morals, ethics and principles can we use?

Religion has been an important factor in the establishment of our standards, but it does not seem to have the force, the impact and the credibility that it traditionally had. Certainly, more people are going through the church doors. But when they come out...???

Some have come to the conclusion that religious codes have some groundwork in superstition. And it is so true. We are told by some denominations that if we sin, we will be damned in hell fire. Pictures are then shown of the devil armed with a fork tormenting sinners in a furnace. Mortal sins will see you safely into hell, while a lesser sin, (venial sin) will see you into a limbo or a purgatory (some kind of temporary prison)! When I was younger, this one used to bother me because I always wanted to know how long one had to stay locked up for one small, little venial sin.

Needless to say, all answers by informed Catholic 'experts' (priests and religion teachers etc.) to my questions were well spiced with "Ah....", "Well, ah, you know... ah", "It depends", and "If... well... ah..."!

In the Dark ages these 'threats' and 'judgments' worked extremely well. They kept most people pious meek and mild, submissive and hugely superstitious. However, these 'threats' and 'intimidatory' statements hold little water among young people today... and some older ones too! Most people, except when confronted with insurmountable problems, terminal illnesses or imminent death are not overly concerned with their after-life.

They are mostly concerned with their here-and-now life! Thus, we find ourselves in a position where some of us, particularly the younger majority, are searching for a new and different moral order.

Is this necessary?

Behind us we have great teachers – in words and deeds! Lao Tzu, Confucius, Moses, Isaiah, Job, Socrates, Plato, Buddha, Aristotle, Jesus Christ, St. Paul, Mohammed, Martin Luther and a host of others. What did they teach? What did they emphasize?

They taught that the person must seek to develop him/herself to make the best of this experience of life, to live according to certain very basic principles, to search for the true self within, to seek harmony with the Divine Spirit which prevails in this world, and to develop and grow physically, mentally, socially and spiritually.

In our search for an acceptable code of moral principles, we must examine their teachings, we must explore within our inner minds and we must let our findings guide our actions.

A NEW CODE OF MORALS? - *PART 2*

Published in The Workers' Voice March 15th 1983

Basically, when we think of morality, we think of two principles: good or bad. Thus we classify our actions and those of others in one or the other category. Speaking indecent language or the public exhibition of sexual acts are examples that fall into the 'bad' category. Going to church or helping an old person to cross the street are both placed in the 'good' category.

We must be careful, however, when we categorize certain types of behaviours in this way. The person who helps the aged individual across the street could be doing it for selfish or hypocritical reasons (e.g. social or political mileage). Therefore, let us not look at the actions to determine the moral classification. Instead let us look at the inner reasons from which these actions originated so that we can get a truer evaluation. But, can one person do this for another? No! So, let us make this a personal exercise.

Judge Yourself

I propose that our primary challenge today is not to provide more food for tomorrow, or to secure a particular ideology for parties or for demigods; and it is not to make the most money and stash it away either.

Our primary challenge is education: To teach the principles, ethics and values which will make individuals search for divine truths; to teach how individuals can face whatever hardships which tomorrow may bring; and most importantly – to learn one's true purpose in life.

Anyone who feels that hoarding money, that acquiring and amassing huge amounts of property, and the seizing or maintaining of political power will act as buffers between themselves and the momentous times of the future should remember the great flood. As a matter of fact, if we were to make any attempt at classification, these acts would certainly be categorized as 'bad'.

Some ethics and principles must be self taught. The concerned person must listen to the 'intuitive whisperings of the inner mind', otherwise called our 'conscience'.

Though I stress the responsibility of the self for good moral conduct, I am not in any way relieving the society of its role. Indeed, we have two areas of moral responsibility: to ourselves and to the society. Traditionally, the society has been full protected by such moral codes of behavior as those included in the Ten Commandments.

People are different, we do things differently, we perceive things differently, and we feel differently. If we are to be guided by any moral code, it must be one which means the same things to all of us – be it Russian or Chinese, Cuban or American, Swahili or Africaan, Patios or English. If we are truly in search of a life free from baseless superstitions, free from wars of attrition, and free from the increasingly high cost of living, we must adopt a different and more universal approach.

Do not steal your neighbour's property because you would not want him or anyone else to take yours. All of our great teachers support principles like this one. Morality cannot be based on a materialistic philosophy like 'capitalism'.

The individual who finds no value in life other than accumulating wealth and power, will never find and never reflect a moral code that will be stable. His thoughts, speech and actions will reflect values which shift with moods and situations.

Our society as a whole reflects some of this behaviour. Even our legal system is not immune to this when we see justice being determined on the basis of which political, social or institutional framework the defendant or plaintiff is a member of.

Have you ever wondered why even after attaining so much material possessions, and political or financial power, our modern pharaohs, party kings, parliamentary barons, political demigods and mercantile dukes and lords cannot find happiness? If you, the reader fall into one of these categories, how much of your time is spent worrying about keeping what you have and thinking about hiding your minor and/or major indiscretions – and keeping them hidden?

On the other hand, how much time do you get to read a book (not an accounts ledger), going to the beach, taking a stroll, talking to the kids, watching the stars on a clear cloudless night, meditating on life and its principles – getting in tune with yourself?

In the final analysis, your personal happiness will decide which category of morals you utilize. If money and material possessions bring you joy... then make sure you get them while observing the Golden Rule.

Why? Because 'peace of mind' is the only true evidence of physical, material and spiritual health and wealth.

And, 'peace of mind' will be the result of you searching for and finding, applying and keeping a 'new moral code' that serves both you and the society in which you live.

POSITIVE THINKING

Published March 21, 1983

Millions of people have adopted a way of life filled with
negative thinking. We are all susceptible to this kind of
thinking, but there are some who are constantly thinking
negatively. We sometimes magnify our problems way out of
proportion. We feel that we are victims of forces beyond our
control when we are really victims of our negative thoughts.
This creates self pity and the feeling that we are being
persecuted by others – at home, at work and on the
streets.

This kind of thinking is not only bad for our own physical and
mental health, it also makes life difficult for those with whom
we associate.

Another form of negative thinking is laziness. Socrates, the
Greek philosopher, once said, "He is not only idle who does
nothing, but he is idle who might be better employed."

Laziness is often the result of monotony, doing the same thing
over and over. Mental laziness can be the result of thinking
the same kinds of thoughts everyday. An active and alert mind
needs new thoughts and ideas to keep it alive and stimulated.
Killing time is another form of laziness… and it is wasted
energy. This has nothing to do with purposeful relaxation
which is extremely beneficial if one is to live a balanced life.

Creative thinking is the ability to bring forth new ideas which
will assist in solving our day to day problems. It is thinking

on a higher level – free of trivialities and negative thoughts. "The ability to think is the birth right of every individual" is a philosophical concept that has been passed down through the ages. Every thought, action and experience influences us in some way, shaping our character and directing our paths. Study, contemplation and meditation are aids to our total development. Thinking requires that we exercise the mind lest it become stagnant rusty and begins to deteriorate.

Our mind is a very powerful instrument which we should seek to use in a positive and practical way. We cannot allow others to do our thinking for us, but we must pave our own paths to self-illumination and self-mastery in order to achieve whatever goals we have set for ourselves.

Each of us has certain dormant faculties within us. We have the potential to become whatsoever we will or choose. It is through the process of creating, that humankind has made all of the giant steps in modern inventions and scientific achievements.

"You are what you think!" If you think small – you will be small. When you think of losing, if you are filled with doubts and lack of faith and confidence in yourself – then your life will reflect these negative thoughts, your problems will be endless, you will make enemies and you will lose friends and loved ones. You will be quarrelsome, impatient, overly critical and unfriendly. Blood pressure, heart disease, ulcers and headaches will be your constant companions.

Clear away the cobwebs from your mind. What benefits have you received from such negative thoughts? Do you receive perverse pleasure in being sick, lonely, or unhappy? You have the right to develop yourself. Start thinking positively and open the door to a new world and a NEW YOU!

Let us share with each other, even if it is only ideas that we share. Maybe, we too can start a trend in a positive direction in the best interest of humanity.

A Healthy Society - *Part 1*

Published September 15th 1983

Many religious leaders agree that the modern society is sick. Some environmentalists, humanists, philosophers and social scientists agree that something is radically wrong. Indeed, if we listen to the daily news of rapes, murders, political and industrial unrests, diseases, suicides and the host of other conditions, we ourselves will definitely begin to wonder if the society is sick!

The term 'sick' implies a subnormal condition suggesting a departure from a standard or norm which is considered healthy. What then are some factors that tend to destroy a healthy society?

The first element of a healthy society is co-operation. This consists of the 'collective' working together of people toward a common objective. If the society is 'healthy' its united activity must be of a certain quality. The quality of this united activity must be determined by 'freedom'.

Involvement in the activity must be freely motivated and it must not be the result of any militant force contrary to the will of the people involved in the activity. No small group of people should determine what is good for the majority.

This freedom is of a dual nature. On one hand the individual must have the freedom to participate in the decision making process and then involvement in the creative and productive activity. On the other hand, society depends on the unity of agreement and action of its members for its existence.

Does this freedom of the individual grant him the right to attack the freely agreed upon decision of the majority of the people?

History has proven that a majority's decision in society is not always right. Yet, we can exist only if the society as a whole works towards specific ends. However, in any 'healthy' society, the individual should have the freedom of speech and action to disagree with the provisions of the existing social structure.

The expression of diverse ideas and actions by influencing members of society to adopt different concepts and objectives and rational persuasion are means to achieve this type of freedom. However, an exercise of force to protect the individual's or small group's freedom cannot be permitted to obstruct the collective will of the majority.

Thus if we look at the coups and counter coups, assassinations, political repression, political imprisonment, civil wars, anarchists and dictatorships which characterize world society today, we must face the fact that our world society is indeed sick. If we are aware of the misuse and abuse of power by political, religious and industrial leaders then we ourselves ought to feel sick.

Our financial, social, psychological, environmental, educational and physical health depends on our awareness of the present conditions and our ability to change these conditions for the positive development of our society.

Let us look beneath the superficial 'dressing' of our wounds and see if our political, social and religious surgeons have done a skilful, thoughtful, thorough and competent professional job. What is the prognosis? Are we going to survive or are we going to continue to be anemic, malnourished, hypertensive, cancerous and waste away slowly?

Let us be ever watchful that 'we are the ones' in society who must retain health and remain well. Be careful that our 'elected' doctors do not 'bewitch' us into believing that we are well while they compile their fees, spoils and ill-gotten, unhealthy gains!

A Healthy Society - Part 2

Published in the Tribune — September 17ᵗʰ 1983

... Where policy decisions are made not because of practicality or necessity for public good, but because of the next election...

Like cells in the human body, there must be in society a unity of purpose and action. Each individual cannot go off on a journey of thought and action for no other reason than to exhibit personal and unrestricted freedom. This can be, for some, a challenge to self-discipline. In essence, the question asked is: "Why not resort to the full gratification of the appetites and passions?" "The good is pleasure and true value is life!" In ancient times this was called hedonism.

In today's terms it is called permissiveness.

Everyday we hear of changes. The long list includes issues which change the basic microstructure on which our society has so far survived. Suddenly, change has become a positive word without any negative connotation.

Even the Bible has been changed and every rule and law therein has been subjected to billions of interpretations. This has led to the confusion which churches use so well to win members like politicians use to win votes. A society which will remove golden, nucleic standards for the sake of 'openness and change' will definitely enter Grave Street with Sodom and Gomorrah as 'avant-garde'.

In resorting to permissiveness, the individual is rejecting ethical and moral codes of attitude sanctioned by society. Due to the powerful influence of some individuals and some small splinter groups, our society is changing many of the golden standards which once protected it.

The fundamental purpose of morality is to give dominance of those qualities which transcend man's animal nature. Morality, then leads to a refinement of the human being, a transcendence from base sensuality.

Moral precepts are a guide to the equity of human rights. They seek to prevent exploitation of the weak by the strong. With the dizzying increase in the belief that change is inevitable in all areas of modern life and the general decline in the belief that morals are supernatural in origin, immorality has been on the increase.

The level of immorality has reached criminal heights. For example, people in elected office are ripping off the society daily – not necessarily by dipping itchy fingers into the till, but by failing to perform their sworn duty, the duty which they begged, cursed, and cried for; the duty which they vowed and promised to fulfill. Yet our communities are worse off… more diseases, more filth… more unemployment.

We are no less to blame for the increase of immorality. Look at Carnival. This has become the time of the year when each of us 'free up ourselves'. Things which are usually sinful, immoral and unethical are all right during our "Summer Festival." No wonder most teenage pregnancies originate at this time. The Carnival Baby is definitely a reality. Gambling is OK at 'Las Vegas' during Carnival – only at Carnival!

Are these signs of a healthy society?

Today, most of the standards which were known and accepted by our grandparents are only vague memories attributed to the senile conscience. When morals change, roles must change, and attitudes and behaviours also change. New frontiers replace the old. Crime, violence and freedom to physically attack anyone because it is a 'just cause' is allowed international respectability.

Out of the basic need for its continue existence, society imposes certain responsibilities on each person. These are of two general types. The first is universal, that is, it is applied alike to all members of society. The other kind of responsibility varies with the individual's skills and capabilities. There is, however, a growing reluctance of individuals to share their responsibilities in meeting the burdens of society.

This 'irresponsibility' can be seen in classrooms, where some teachers act as if the job is too big for them. It can be seen in government offices where clerks are lethargic and their supervisors are unwilling to make decisions. Even worse it can be seen at the top, where policy decisions are made not because of practicality or necessity for the public good, but because of the 'next' elections.

This kind of attitude is unhealthy because it degrades the credibility of the political office and places the elected official in disrepute. It humiliates and shames those who voted and placed confidence in their party. These conditions then give rise to discontent, vexation and disillusionment. Workers become frustrated then lethargic, exigent then indifferent. And then, the dark clouds of unhealthy attitudes begin to settle over the nation. Unhealthy public attitudes give rise to an unhealthy society.

In discussing a healthy society one may immediately think of such topics as 'Litter Bills', family life, quality of mental health, number of teenage pregnancies, level of community health care and 'night soils'.

Indeed, we need to be concerned about the standards, practices and statistics relative to these and other issues. We must not only be concerned, but we must act positively and use our freedom of speech. We must ensure that we achieve physical and emotional health in order to ascertain that society's unborn will meet an environment of clean gutters, communities, buildings and streets free from 'night soil' carts, littering rubbish trucks and deadly disease carrying germs.

We must agree, however, that health is mostly a state of mind. Thus, our attitudes and behaviors must reflect this state of mind. The performance of our elected and appointed officials must also echo and mirror our feelings on these issues.

Finally, be your own judge. Look into yourself. What are your thoughts and actions? Remember that you, along with 4 billion other persons make up our human society. Thus, **you** will determine the Health of Our Society.

Twin Island State? Fair Antigua & Redonda!

Published 1983

Our State is known as Antigua and Barbuda
Represented on the Coat of Arms by the deer and pineapple
In the National Anthem, the make up of this two island
country
    Is stated clearly
Along with the need to "Dwell in love and unity."

Amid all the clamour about independence negotiations and
discussions
Barbudans, historically forgotten, some even thought of
secession,
And tried unsuccessfully to loosen the knots
    that tied them to Antigua's bottom...
        not bosom.

But, not wanting to lose face
We, like the colonial graspers who still decide our fate,
Held on with the hope of exploiting that little place...
    Rumours of oil, peanuts, sugar-apple farms and hotels,
    sand mines, lobsters, fish and Aragonian brothels -
Were rampant throughout the land
So there were all kinds of shuffling and dealing -
    by many who must have had their heads in the sand...
    with all kinds of schemes, mischievous and devious
    thought up by men with outstretched hands...
        open above and under the table...
    by those money grabbing widdy widdy bush politicians.

Meanwhile, our little sister,
    a name on the map, on Government documents
        - sister only on paper,
Gets left behind in all the planning
    "Each endeavouring, all achieving"???
What mockery! What ridiculous stupidity!!!
Can we really say, for example
Antigua & Barbuda Sports Division?
    No! Never!
Which cricketer, footballer, netball player, athlete or team
    from Barbuda ever took part in a national competition?
But then... we all suffer from Antiguanism!

Have we encouraged and licensed their total development?
    No!
It cannot happen if it's not controlled by an Antiguan
Department...
    Pushed here... pulled there,
Why was there no Carnival for Barbuda this year?
Ah well... there was next to none even over here!
Barbuda cannot be treated like Bendals Village,
    Forgotten, spited, underdeveloped -
It s not yours to plunder, to pillage for spoils and pilferage!

And while Barbudans get left behind,
Discarded, neglected, rejected, all their efforts thwarted,
    put in quicksand, soaked in brine,
Antiguans stand idly by – disinterested,
    comfortable, peaceful, everything O.K. – just fine
Content to argue about Space Research and South Africa
    Angola, Grenada, Communism and Cuba,
Upset maybe about Cricket and some questionable dollars,
    Reagan and his policy towards El Salvador and
Nicaragua.
Shame on you!
What about our backyard – our own backward-ed Barbuda!

Everytime you see the Coat of Arms and the Flag
And each time you sing the National Anthem,
When you reach "Fair Antigua and _____"
Leave that space Blank or maybe say "Redonda"

We are not worthy of calling the name of that left behind land!
I listen to ABS Radio and TV – day and night,
Nothing said or seen of our 'sister' island..
    What a plight!
Again they are forgotten – there is no justice,
But then the initials A.B.S.
    Stands for Antigua Broadcasting Service!
If Barbuda represents problems without solutions,
Then, for heavens sake, give them their freedom
    To decide their future,
    To take themselves our of this destitute situation,

Hands in hand, let us all rise to this decision,
Either or, forget about power and politics,
Be humane, be reasonable, put aside ideological differences…
    We are talking about people – not systems.
Their lives, their future, the health of their children
Must take priority over any personal "belonging to" sentiments
For
They are not ours – they belong to themselves only
Why not?
Let them Barbudans take charge of their own destiny!

NEGOTIATIONS

Published in the Antigua Business News, March 1984

The business world today is characterized by problems such as those in the areas of finance, marketing, purchasing, labour relations, production and management. More than ever before, experts are searching for potential people with the specific skills which are needed to tackle these problems. The art of effective negotiating is emerging as one of the foremost skills required.

The term 'negotiating' suggests a two-way communication in decision-making, conflict resolution, trading or exchanging, and collective bargaining. Ideally, negotiating occurs in an atmosphere of positive cooperation and trust with the expressed intention of satisfying everyone. Thus, the idea of giving to get and the spirit of compromise are both integral parts of any negotiating effort.

The practice of negotiating has existed for as long as humans have been interacting with each other. The processes involved in dealing with business, political, social and, particularly, military conflicts have emerged in the modern day from ancient times. Negotiating has served as a social strategy to reduce conflict between communities and individuals so that the 'society at large' can get on with the business of living. Of course, when I think of the word 'negotiating', I also think of the word 'bargaining'. This really sets the process of coming to an agreement in its proper historical context, since 'bargaining' was essentially the first type of selling. Everyone learned how to bargain for the best deal.

In today's business world, the concept of bargaining has evolved but the primary underpinning goal is the same: Two parties try to come to a common agreement on a specific and clearly identified matter.

In bargaining or negotiating, differences of opinion will occur, but this does not automatically imply conflict. According to one expert, the objective is "not to widen or breach relationships" but, "to build and to create better on-going relationships." Both parties should be satisfied. There should be "no winners or losers," and, "everyone should emerge winners."

Whether the activity includes hiring, purchasing, arranging loans, renting, selling or conciliating, or whenever people are involved in the communication process for change, both the communication and negotiation process should be positive. The whole idea is to achieve meaningful cooperation.

Thus, the negotiating process should never be used as an 'offensive diplomatic' tool or weapon for the achievement of organizational, systemic or personal gains. For this, in itself, would be a breach of trust. And, any sign or indication of any such breach should be totally condemned.

More importantly, the negotiation process should not be used to achieve goals or objectives by organizations, parties or individuals who are outside of the parties to the process! Third parties should have no influence on any aspect of the process. The outcome of the process should not be at the mercy of any organization or institution... be it private, government or the church, or whether it is thought that the matter has social, political or religious implications!

As a matter of fact, as I understand it, when there is evidence of purposefully improper representation or fraudulent misrepresentation, any negotiation settlement reached on such circumstance can be set aside legally. Here the principle of 'good faith' seems to be applied! Of course, these days we see little, if any evidence, of faith. Most of what we see is – well – 'good fraud'!

The question arises therefore, as to the intentions of the parties. Are there hidden third parties who are attempting to the influence the outcome? Is there hidden pressure? Are there hidden agendas? This is particularly crucial in Caribbean and Antigua and Barbuda labour relations, where persons involved in the negotiating process have demonstrated and expressed motives other than fair settlement of the questions or issues in any particular issue.

These motives serve to cloud, confuse, and perplex the negotiating process. Issues with normally simple and general alternatives and possibilities and which usually would have been solved through responsible representation, now develop into monstrous conflicts, fed and fanned into political and ideological flames by selfishly motivated and repeatedly rejected would-be politicians.

Negotiations are usually settled on statistical evidence, incidents of precedents, natural law and justice, and fair consideration on all aspects of the arguments presented. Here again, the expressed intention should be to be fair and just to those involved in the issue, for example: workers and management.

The idea is not and should never be to negotiate in order to enhance the political or professional image of the persons or organizations representing the parties. The process should be focused on the expressed desires of the parties that are being represented. This calls for trust and for ethical and responsible behaviours by the various negotiating teams.

Improper motives and practices usually force negotiations from 'around the table' to the very ineffective conciliation level, up to the questionable arbitration level and then on to the very cumbersome, time-consuming and time stealing judicial level. Even at some levels of the conciliation process, one can see evidence of other considerations sneaking in through meaningless rhetoric by legally empowered official third parties.

Is it any wonder that there is congestion, confusion and stagnation in Antigua and Barbuda's labour relations process?

THE PROFIT MOTIVE

January 17ᵗʰ 1985

Harry says, "The profit motive in business has produced rapid progress, increased productivity, inventions and innovations, and a better quality of life for all."

Karen replies, "How can you say that? Just look around. The profit motive has actually produced or increased poverty, slums, pollution, greed corruption, social inequities, economic instability and a host of other problems."

There is some truth in Harry's statement. But Karen's reply certainly, in my mind, stands out as the more correct based on the realities of people's lives from all around the world.

Unquestionably, the profit motive in business has always existed. Before banks and multinational corporations came into being, the grain traders of the Steppes, the jade dealers of Canton, the fur traders of Lapland and the Phoenicians of the Mediterranean were all busily involved in turning a profit. However, business was usually conducted on the basis of mutual agreement and satisfaction of the parties, and most goods were produced and supplied on a needs basis. The trader of the Pampas lowlands had wool which was needed in the high Andes. He traded for gold which was plentiful in the mountains and which was more highly regarded in the lowland villages and towns. The townspeople then traded their newly obtained gold for clothes and finery imported from foreign lands.

With the advent of the 18th Century Industrial Revolution, however, the concept of supply and demand changed and took on different forms. New markets had to be created for the goods developed by increased production output. Production of goods was not to fulfill demands… was not according to the needs of society, but to satisfy the need of the producer to get increased profits; hence the profit motive.

This led to aggressive sales and marketing strategies and inhuman and immoral methods of increasing and sustaining production cheaply. These methods included the trading of Africans for the sole purpose of increasing cotton and sugar production in the West Indies, and North and South America. Added to African slavery were other strategies such as indentured servitude and shanghaiing people, and paying workers inhumanely low wages. Other techniques such as control of production levels and price fixing by major companies ensured that products or their parts would always be in high demand.

The fact that economists support the concept that business exists to serve mankind is nothing short of a bad joke.

Business exists to make a profit – nothing else. Any side effects are incidental and serve to bolster the image of the business concern. There is even a tactic these days where businesses are able to escape taxation: corporations give money to not-for-profit organizations so that they can get "tax shelters", create better public image, become good corporate citizens, boost their marketing promotions through these 'community' efforts… and thereby increase their profits.

The vast majority of companies determine that they must make the most profit – by any means necessary. This might mean polluting oceans, having landfills

overflow poor villages, or manufacturing and marketing dangerous products.

The *profit motive* has historically led to the creation of new markets. No longer was Indian silk traded with countries in the Indian Ocean region; it was needed in England. The whole world was the new market place. This of course led to new and innovative inventions in every arena of life: communications and travel, vehicles and machines, architecture and work, technology and innovations in industry. The world would never be the same again.

Certainly, the new inventions and technological innovations can be called progress. But they certainly did not bring a better quality of life for all.

The profiteers were profiting! But the masses of workers, indentured servants, shanghaied innocents, and black slaves were, if anything, in a worse dilemma.

In the case of the slaves, for example, they were dragged, chained head, hands and feet into rat infested cestpool slavers (ships) and carried thus to another land, where they were cruelly sold by public auction – *for profit* – into – not only a lifetime of slavery – but generations of slavery. All to support, to nourish the budding concept of 18th and 19th century business and trade profit – the birth of the capital economy.

Due to the profit motive, many countries and continents (for example, America and Australia) were invaded by hosts of land grabbing immigrants who raped, tortured, killed, plundered and thereby subdued the natives who were defenseless in the face of the superior weapons and the genocidal aggressiveness of the new arrivals.

The natives were also defenseless in the face of the onslaught of the Bible toting advance legions of so-called Christian missionaries who preceded or at least accompanied almost every European plunderer of native peoples. In Africa, the plunderers also included Muslim missionary conquerors. In any case, today's descendants of those natives cannot catch themselves and have not yet recovered. Not to this day! Maybe never! Examples of this can be found everywhere – all over North America, South America, Australia and everywhere south of the equator!

Today, even though the quality of life has improved a little for a precious few, most natives of these countries are dirt poor, malnourished and suffer the social nightmares of victimization, segregation, discrimination and economic exclusion as a direct result of more than two hundred years of aggressive plundering driven by the profit motive.

Certainly, poverty and slums have always existed. But with the increase in affluence in some countries and regions of the world, one would have thought that poverty would have decreased in a statistically significant way. Instead, there is now more starvation and famine in the world today than ever before. The continent of Africa has been stripped almost bare of its natural wealth by the European colonial profiteers. Many of its countries have been left as bare as the ageless rocks and sands of the Sahara Desert. Its resources – gold and other precious metals, diamonds and even oil - have been ripped out of its belly and placed in the bosom of Europe and America.

Where wealth still exists in these countries, it is controlled by the sons and daughters of the first sets of profiteers who stayed behind to control the 'economic interests' of their forbears. Thus, the natives are either economic slaves in their own lands or totally at the mercy of foreign investors, the World Bank, or the 'global companies'.

The profit motive has not only produced poverty – it continues to encourage, support and sustain it – to the detriment of native peoples and disadvantaged populations everywhere.

It is for profit, and only for profit, why the American Government, the British Parliament, the German Bundestag and the Japanese Nyet will not even verbally discourage South Africa's Apartheid policy.

It is for the profit of its business companies that America intervenes – with a wink of approval from its European allies and Canada – in the internal affairs of countries such as Cuba or tiny Grenada.

Figures released by the World Bank in 1982 showed that 65% of the world's population are living in abject poverty; 15% are barely above that margin, while a small 20% control all the wealth. Furthermore, of the latter 20%, 2% was making all the important decisions and controlled 80% of the world's resources.

On their way to the accumulation of large fortunes, the two percent - the multi-national profiteers, those greedy modern-day pirates whose God is the dollar sign ($), have destroyed not only the will and hope of the average human, they have carelessly polluted the environment.

Of course… profiteers profit by any means necessary. It cannot be disputed that the levels of environmental pollution which have today reached disastrously high and nightmarish proportions, are the direct results of the uncompromising drive of the profit motive. Whole classes of animals have been destroyed for fur, horn or skin. The face of the land has been so scarred that it has even affected the earth's weather pattern. Factories emit so much poisonous smoke in the air that we and future generations will have to contend with acid rain and other climactic challenges and as a direct result... untold millions will suffer.

Corruption among officials of these profit driven enterprises is the norm: finding loopholes in Government laws is the primary job of lawyers and financiers; promoting unhealthy life damaging foods and other dangerous commodities such as drugs, alcohol and cigarettes is the unconcerned duty of our media. And why? Only for Profit. The profiteers rule supreme. The hunt for money – by any means necessary – is at the root of their evil.

Social inequity is a fact of daily life. On a village level, a city level, nationally and internationally. Society is divided into classes – the rich and the poor; the haves and the have nots. There are only two levels – rich and poor. Those in between – who aspire to join the rich class... are usually the ones who do the dirty work for the privileged.

And the poor have no chance of changing their status: you are born poor- you will die poor. And this is a dilemma we face today in a world where there is enough food to be shared, and enough resources which would make every human comfortable.

Countries like the United States and Canada have huge reserves of food which from time to time are destroyed as the 'over supplies' grow. Why are over-supplies destroyed... Because too much food and the prices will be lowered... Too little food and the prices will increase. Supply... and demand. Create the demand and reduce the supply... key economic principles driven by the profit motive. Meanwhile... millions die in Africa each year from famine and malnutrition. Even more horrible and totally reprehensible is the fact that there are millions of people in America itself who do not know where the next meal is coming from and who live on the streets and eat from garbage cans competing with back ally dogs, cats and rats. Why can't these resources – these reserves – be given freely to those who need them? Well: There is no profit involved in almsgiving.

From the foregoing we can see that the profit motive in business has in fact produced rapid progress in the area of technological innovations and inventions but it has not produced a better quality of life for all. Instead it has fostered greed and corruption, bred slavery, promoted and protected apartheid, encouraged inequities, decimated whole populations of human beings and plant life – and endangered the future of earth.

The profit motive raises serious questions about the whole economic structure on earth. Why should 2% of the population control 80% of the earth's resources? Why in this age of great technological progress should millions of people be suffering from famine, political wars and be made third class citizens, virtually slaves in their own native lands?

Not only is the structure of the world economy in question but its foundation, the whole concept itself, and the underlying principles must be examined. Should not businesses exist, not for the enlightened few, but for the upliftment, enhancement and illumination of the masses? Shouldn't the labourer in the pits, threatened by real danger to his life, be as highly paid as the executive whose only fear is the loss of his job? And who needs profits more – the Fords of America or the tribesmen from Botswana?

These issues must be quickly dealt with because it is felt by many that the profit motive will eventually result in a few cancerous corporations or their host nations spreading their tentacles and holding the rest of humankind to ransom. The earth and all of its resources will eventually not only be threatened but face destruction.

This I predict is around the corner. And, we will all suffer.

Even the profiteers.

THE ANTIGUA HUSTLE

Published in "The Caribbean Sun" Newspaper, Washington, DC. March 1987

Papa Bird   A hero of sorts
               From the post war era
               A contemporary of Bradshaw, Williams and
               Manley, Bustamante, Burnham and Crompton
               Even of Bishop, Seaga, Simmonds, Robinson
                        and of course, Adams and Barrow

And still   Captain of the HMS/US Antigua
               A veteran of laudable campaigns
                        to win freedom for his country
               Now clinging to his seat
                        of power
               And facing the threat of a Cabinet mutiny

Antigua   A Parliament with all representatives
                        from one party
               Elected by an overwhelming majority
                        A license for all activities?
               Ministers, long accused of corruption
               As evidenced by the latest scandal
                        An older one of papa's sons
               Accused by the French Government
                        of "mishandling" US$11 Million
               For an airport project that some claim
                        cost only a "few hundred thousand"!

The Politicians Of the "ruling" party
        Fighting among themselves for the top
           position to be vacated by Bird,
           senior – since he is getting older…
        Voluntary or by the will of his maker
        The No. 1 contender? Baby Bird – Lester
           Yet – Not automatic
        Since others (Harris, Freeland and St. Luce)
           And even the older brother,
        Pose serious threats to a Lester "take over"!

The Other Parties
        Divided – only a thread of serious opposition
        Disorganized, irresolute, insecure, indecisive
           No definiteness of purpose!
        No clear goals; no meaningful alternate
           programs
           They lack vision!
        Yet, that threat can only be sown
           If combined with ACLM
        The needle that has been pricking the Bird
           Blimp over the past ten years
        Socialist, though, it stands a little chance
           Maybe…
        Since ALL other politicians rote Reagan's
           communist bogey fears.

The Climate Surface level – hustling and bustling,
        The appearance of plenty to do,
           Business seemingly thriving.
        Sure, for Italian, American and Englishmen,
           Buying up all the local lands,
         Syrians and Lebanese – competing with local
           entrepreneurs
        They, locals, constantly ignored by foreign
           owned banks

We dependent on tourism – fragile at best
People work half a year, then idle during the
rest

And them claim – zero unemployment ....
Them got glaucoma,
And them claim, we will soon import foreign
workers
Madness...

The People   Disillusioned, bewildered by the political
chaos,
In a state of apathy – uncaring
Benumbed by scandalous behavior of officials,
Nowhere to turn, no alternative leadership!
Sure, a spend thrift spirit exists,
TV's, clothes, jewelry
All outstripped by expensive motor cars
But this underlines the country's woes,
Cause – when you buy one today
Then, tomorrow them foreign banks –
forecloses!

The Future   Holds important developments
As there are powerful undercurrents...
of political cleansing
Note – Haiti – to some degree
And Trinidad – which got rid of the entrenched
party
As Barbadians called for liberalization,
So will Jamaica – turn to less of the World
Bank and to that US Reagan

Antigua   For certain – those Cabinet reshuffles
Will not stem the flow of ministers' illegal
hustles

Nor can political retreats
Cleanse the minds of the corrupt
Only people power can...
And...
Them must soon wake up!

IN HIS FOOTSTEPS

January 29th, 1995

Little boys in Sierra Leone, Sudan, Somalia ... all over Africa
Little boys in Palestine, Afghanistan, Iraq and Sri Lanka
In the world's battlegrounds with deadly weapons placed in
their hands
Forced to fight in wars they don't... can't ever understand...

A Little boy... cultured to be his own enemy...
Preventing himself from maturing and raising a family...
Committing atrocities against humanity...
No hope for him... no hope for him... Even in paternity
His baby will likely follow in the steps of his daddy...

Little boys from Jamaica and Argentina to Calcutta, India
Little boys from the Bronx and Brixton to Pristina, Kosova
On the street corners pushing deadly drugs – meth, heroin and
cocaine
Lured into illegal activities that kill and maim their own again
and again

A Little boy... cultured to be his own enemy...
Preventing himself from maturing and raising a family...
Committing atrocities against humanity...
No hope for him... Even in the possibility of his paternity
His baby will likely follow in the steps of his daddy...

Little boys from Washington, DC to Bogota, Colombia
Little boys from Brazil, Mexico and South Africa
Failing in school, forming gangs, burying their future
possibilities

They seem to be clueless about their social and spiritual
responsibilities

A Little boy... cultured to be his own enemy...
Preventing himself from maturing and raising a family...
Committing atrocities against humanity...
No hope for him... no hope for him... Even in paternity
His baby will likely follow in the steps of his daddy...

Little boys from east to west and from the mountain top to the
valley
Little boys from north to south and from the rivers to the sea
I think they are unconsciously hurting and in deep pain
What can I as an adult man do to help them become more
humane?

A Little boy... *not wanting* to be his own enemy...
He desires to mature and grow and raise a family...
In his despair he yearns to be an integral and positive part of
humanity...
He hopes and dreams that if not he – then the fruits of his
paternity
His baby will not follow in the footsteps of his daddy...

Transformation from the Inside... Out

Thursday, December 02, 2004

The word "**Transformation**" suggests changing something from one thing to another... from one state of being to another state of being; it suggests creating something new from something old... it suggests moving across and over and through boundaries and obstacles in order to form new realities, new skills, new competencies, new products and new services.

In order for transformation - whether personal, social or organizational to occur, I propose that a radical shift in mindsets, in thinking, in the mental models of the people involved must occur.

The key here is that in order for transformation to occur on the outside - this radical shift must occur on the inside. Not inside families, or societies or organizations - but within the hearts and minds - feelings and thoughts - of each individual.

Transformation - whether within organizations, communities, families or individuals - **starts within each individual - from the inside... and then to the outside.**

EDUCATIONAL DATA

By Marcus M. Mottley, Ph.D

On Saturday, February 25th 2005, Bill Gates blasted the state of U.S. high schools in a speech before the National Association of Governors Education Summit in the Washington, DC.

Listening to Gates on C-Span, I was compelled to compare his concerns about the state of education in America to my own concern about the state of education in Antigua and Barbuda.

Gates said that he was "ashamed" and "appalled" at the failure rates for students. He called America's high schools broken, flawed and under-funded, and said the system itself is obsolete. Gates comments were fueled by the fact that "statistics" showed that when compared to twenty other 'developed' nations (mainly European countries) American education ranked quite low in most areas.

I struggled to compare our education with that of any other country outside the Caribbean. Why? Because, while educational 'statistics' are easily obtainable in any district or state in America, getting information on our students in Antigua and Barbuda is downright difficult – if not almost impossible. 'Difficult' because what ever little data have been collected, they are not easily available or accessible. 'Almost impossible' because a lot of the data have not been collected and collated to be made sense of and then reported!

I could fill this article with hundreds of questions that have been burning within me for years. Questions for which, many of my friends in education have had either no answers to, avoided, or presented circuitous, pathetic, 'shameful', 'appalling' and at best, poor defensive retorts.

Here are a few questions: What is the reading level of students who enter First Form in our secondary schools? And, by the way, is there a way to measure the level those students are reading at? What percentage of them need remedial work in mathematics (or Reading, Writing, or English) when they first enter the secondary education system? How many of the students who enter First Form graduate on time? Which Form do they tend to repeat the most? How many graduate at all?

Do we have data on all students and in all schools as they move from grade to grade or from form to form? In other words, can and do we track students from the time they enter the formal educational system until they graduate (or drop out)? By the way, what are our drop-out rates? I mean the 'real figures'? For those who drop out… what propels them to leave? Is it age, poor academic results, poverty and family pressure to work, drug and alcohol use, gangs, negative peer pressure, pregnancy, or just a lack of motivation to complete their education?

How many post-primary students graduate on time? Are they tracked differently from those students who enter the secondary school at First Form? What general difficulties do the Post Primary Students have and in which subject areas do they have problems? Are these problems different from their peers who entered directly into First Form?

What does graduation mean anyway? Does it mean that a student has 'completed' Fifth Form? Or, does it mean that the student has successfully met a pre-determined standard of achievement? And, what is this standard of achievement and how is it measured?

When a student enters the secondary level, what ought to be his/her *minimum* goals for success at 'graduation'? Should it be to pass five CXC subjects at a certain level? Should it be to 'just get through' 5th Form – that being the key to attend the 'graduation ceremony'? Or should there be something else? What does 'get through' mean? Does it mean that the student reached 5th Form, stayed in 5th Form until the end of the school year… even though he or she did not pass any subjects?

If the standard of achievement is taking the CXC Examinations, then what is the standard of achievement that says to a student: "You have successfully met the minimum requirements to be designated as a 'Secondary School Graduate'"? And, if such a student has met those minimum requirements for 'graduation'… should that student not get a Secondary School Diploma from the Ministry of Education?

I have presented in this article, a few of the many questions that I and many others need answers to. The intention here is not criticize but to critique, not to impeach but to inspire, not to enrage but to engage our leaders in education to look at the deeper issues. My purpose here is to encourage them not only to inform, not only to reform, but to radically transform the Antiguan and Barbuda education system – not the OECS, not CARICOM… but the **Antigua and Barbuda** education system!

ANTIGUANS EMBOLDENED

Saturday, September 10, 2005

"Strike!" "Protest!" These are words that we hear more and more of in Antigua these days. Teachers strike over the lab at All Saints School. Staff at the court strike over working conditions. Teachers are upset because they are called out 'a day early'. Bus and taxi drivers demand a 25% hike in fares.

Are these the results of an empowered populace? Are these the results of having a government that promotes openness (sunshine)?

Or are these the results of people and organizations secretly and clandestinely doing the work of the opposition?

Or are these results an indication that people perceive the Baldwin Spencer Administration to be weak?

Whatever is happening, suddenly Antiguans have suddenly been emboldened to "Strike" and "Protest". Whatever it is, Antiguans are protesting in ways that they never did under the ALP administration.

There are some who indicate that they can see the obvious hand of the ALP behind the leaders of the Teachers Union and the Public Service Commission. There are others who think that the "openness" of the Baldwin Spencer Government is perceived as weakness, indecisiveness, and 'wimpish' leadership.

There are others who think that "openness" and "sunshine" are refreshing elements of the new administration which promote the involvement of the people in the process of governance... something they claim was missing from the previous 28 years of the last administration.

LEADERSHIP ETHICS AT
THE CROSSROADS

Friday, October 28, 2005

According to Warren Bennis and Bert Nanus, "Trust is the emotional glue that binds followers and leaders together." I propose that this is at the heart of why I think that 'leadership ethics' is at a crossroads.

Do we have leaders, in Antigua and Barbuda, who are worthy of our trust, fully committed to our interests and who share our values? Do we have leaders who we can trust will pursue goals that make our current conditions better and lead to a brighter and more solid future for our children? Do we have leaders whose activities are firmly rooted in the election promises they make and the expectations they engender from us?

Whether in Antigua or in America... or elsewhere, the truthful answers to those questions are disquieting. An Iraq war that was supposed to be about freeing the world of terrorism has mired that country in debacle after debacle. And the world has suffered directly! You and I pay at the gas pump... because of the Iraq war. Was it about freedom... or was it about control of oil, control of American interests, or payback for threats to a presidential father? In Antigua... the wanton giving-away of the people's lands to American and Asian 'Pirates of the Caribbean'... was it about economic development? Or, was it about personal profit? In Antigua... the debacle called Mount St. John... from which lawyers made millions and, according to popular rumor, politicians (on both sides) seemed to have profited financially – directly and indirectly.

Whether in Antigua, America or elsewhere, as a matter of fact, everywhere – 'leadership ethics' is at a crossroads.

Bernard M. Bass and Paul Steidlmeier of the Center for Leadership Studies, School of Management at Binghamton University in New York, contend that "The ethics of leadership rests upon three pillars: (1) the moral character of the leader, (2) the ethical values embedded in the leader's vision, articulation, and program which followers either embrace or reject, and (3) the morality of the processes of social ethical choices and actions that leaders and followers engage in and collectively pursue." I would argue that of the three pillars that Bass and Steidlmeier identify, the first pillar, "The moral character of the leader" is the most important. It is like a super-pillar on which all other pillars stand. Why? Because in today's world, even in our so-called democracies, the 'leader' is endowed and invested with enormous authority and huge decision-making powers that can impact the lives (and deaths) of thousands of people.

With the stroke of a pen, any one of today's private or public sector leaders, can impact billions of people around the globe. From *President Bush* to *President Chavez*; from *Rex Tillerson*, president of ExxonMobil Corporation to *G. Richard "Rick" Wagoner Jr.* President and CEO of General Motors; from *Steve Hills*, president and general manager of the Washington Post to *Tian Congming*, president of Xinhua News Agency (China News Agency): They all have the power to influence billions of people – positively and negatively.

And, very few of them, seemed inclined to make decisions that are unequivocally in the best interests of the vast populations they either serve or impact. They seemed more inclined to make decisions which serve themselves and the special interests of a select few... rather than the broad majority. As in America... a la Enron and Global Crossing... As in Antigua...

a la Medical Benefit and the so-called Asian Village Project (and many more).

We are at a cross roads of ethical leadership because, while much of the world is apparently moving towards a 'theoretical' democracy, we are increasingly dependent on individuals who ascend to the throne of global power and authority. And, if recent events in both the private and public sectors can be seen as yard sticks, 'followers' (public shareholders and citizen stakeholders) need to be vigilant, cautious and exercise more independence in decision-making. They also need to be less trusting and demand total transparency to spotlight and bring 'sunshine' to the process of public and private sector governance.

What can leaders do? According to Bass and Steidlmeier "modern western philosophy tacitly assumes that there is no morally valid leadership without the consent of the led." Therefore, I think that leaders must remember that one of the central tenets of western philosophy, and indeed, democracy is that all 'all authority emanates from the governed.' Since the weight of ethical leadership rests on the central pillar of the 'moral character of the leader', modern leaders must also embrace the Confucian notion of the 'moral sage' and 'superior person'. This is similar to Plato's idea of the 'philosopher king' whose wisdom and purity allows him or her to rise above base idealism and personal faults like the greed, favoritism, lust and licentiousness we see in many of our political and religious leaders of this age. *(Religious? That's for another post to this blog!)* Leaders must privately uphold the values that they publicly espouse whether these are moral, religious or spiritual traditions and customs. And they must do so by focusing on proper and *right conduct* and behaviors.

The leader who goes to church on Sunday and robs his shareholders on Monday is certainly demonstrating an immoral character – no matter what he says publicly. The leader who argues for a pay raise, in addition to a multiple million dollar salary while he is downsizing his workforce, while his company's profits are down and while shareholders are losing money is definitely demonstrating a greedy character. A leader who preys on the vulnerable within his organization (or country) and coerces or lures them into activities that serve his base interests is demonstrating a character ingrained with lust and depravity.

The moral character of a leader is as important as his visionary ideas, his creative decision-making and his strength in motivating people to embrace a 'shared future' together.

Finally, the western world has promulgated a philosophy where each person is responsible for himself, and every individual pursues his or her own self interest. Seemingly, based on the constant stream of negative examples, today's leaders have passionately embraced this individualism to the exclusion of a leader's commitment to and responsibility to his or her 'followers'. This needs to change.

According to Rawls (1971) the legitimacy of leadership depends on granting the same liberty and opportunity to others that one claims for oneself. The legitimacy of leadership, in America or in Antigua, rests on telling the truth, keeping promises, distributing to each what is due, and employing valid incentives or sanctions.

The legitimacy of leadership rests on developing a vision to make life better for the 'followers' and employing all resources into activities that fulfill that vision: Activities that serve even the poor, the sick, the unemployed, the under-educated, the young and the old; Activities that particularly serve those who are least able now… and who need a hand up… or a hand-out; Activities that motivate stimulate the most able to help up *and* help out the least able; Activities that serve members, followers, critics, and opposers alike!

Leaders who follow these principles recognize not only the pluralism of values and diversity of motivations among their 'followers', but also recognize that he or she exists (in their mantle of leadership) solely to serve the interests of their public shareholders or citizen stakeholders... and not their own.

Leadership is an exercise in the highest form of service: To others!

In Antigua... 'leadership ethics' is at a crossroads. Will the Sunshine Government turn aside or turn back to the corruption of the past? Will it hold true and walk through the difficult roads ahead while keeping to the straight and narrow.

Can we trust that this Government will stay the course and demonstrate high moral character?

How can we tell? Let's not forget the "Agenda for Change!" Remember these phrases? Whistle blower protection! Integrity will be our bedrock! Transparency and accountability will be our watchwords! The Government will be the servants of the people... that is our commitment! The people's purpose will always come first! A people centered agenda!

If we keep the sunlight focused on the above commitments, it will be easy to tell whether or not the UPP leadership has turned aside, turned back or is forging ahead. They are at an ethical crossroads of leadership - right now... and for some it seems as though it is hard not to look back... or at least sideways... And they are signs that some are beginning to slip side-ways into the tempting shadows... at the beckon and behest of privateers and profiteers!

Let's keep them focused… let's help them to look straight ahead… Let's keep the spotlight right above them and around them.

Let's keep the Sunshine Government in the sunshine!

Under the "Big Tent"

Wednesday, October 26, 2005

Prior to the election, the United Progressive Party made an offer to supporters, hangers on, cronies, and fence straddlers attached to the then Labor Party Government. The UPP promised to provide a **"Big Tent"** under which all and sundry could seek shelter.

Since winning the election, they have certainly fulfilled their promise. Everyone in our twin island state can testify that they have kept their promise. No one can question that. Not even the opposition ALP. Particularly not the ALP... since they are, according to all accounts, making political hay while the **"sun shines"**!

And to the great dismay and ire of many life long stalwarts and supporters of the UPP ... their leadership has stuck to *this* campaign promise. Many say that such a commitment will prove to be at least detrimental... and most likely suicidal. Other '**observers**' indicate that while UPP mainstream supporters are deeply upset over this, ALP supporters and officials are apparently quite happy with the "**Tent**" arrangement.

What's happening here?

Well, it seems quite obvious that because the UPP Administration opened its naïve arms to embrace supporters and members of the ALP, it left itself wide open and vulnerable to all kinds of covert and clandestine undermining of its ability to govern. Because of its "Tent" policy, it continues to suffer all kinds of sabotage (overt and covert) at the hands of the supposed 'converts' under the "Tent".

Of course, it is understood that the UPP's leadership wanted to demonstrate that it made a campaign promise... and was committed to fulfilling it (at least this one). But many of their dyed-in-blue supporters are asking... how far are they willing to go to? Will they continue along this road... even to the precipice of self-destruction – at the hands of the surreptitious activities of the so-called "converts to the Tent"?

Our **Government** in the **Sunshine** might find the following commentary insightful. It is a single sentence from a passage written by Yagyu Munenori, master Japanese Swordsman, teacher of the Shogun, and an elder contemporary of the legendary swordsman Musashi (author of the Book of Five Rings). Munenori wrote that, **"The consideration given to the selection of officials and the security of the nation is also an art of war."** (*The Book on Family Traditions in the Art of War.*)

An art of war! *Are we at war?*

I think we are at war.

We are at war against corruption... At war against criminal activities in high office... At war against the theft of the people's resources - including our lands... At war against unethical behaviors by elected and unelected officials and their cronies... many of whom are living happily smirking under the "Tent".

Yes... we are at war. At war against the international 'shame and pain' caused by the last administration (*from the UPP Manifesto*). We are at war against 'an economy in shambles' *(from the UPP Manifesto)*. We are at war against the 'private land bankers' who currently hoard our lands *(from the UPP Manifesto)*. We are at war against the "Pirate of the Caribbean" (I guess that is from **my** Manifesto)! We are at war against the 'vast tracts of land that have been sold off in dubious deals, government ministers and family and friends of the ALP elite *(from the UPP Manifesto)* **many of whom are now protected under the Big Tent of the UPP!** We are at war against the privateers and profiteers who use government money as their private funding source... and who use government officials as their lackeys. Some of these profiteers secure government positions in order to fund and enlarge their rise in one generation from poor greedy immigrants to outlandishly rich greedy immigrant-come-lately-Antiguans.

We are at war! No one can question that. And no one can question that we are at war against issues, situations, and circumstances that were created by people who are not only protected under the **Big Blue (and red) UPP Tent**, but created by people who are also *now* part of the small, inner sanctum of the UPP itself... even at some of the highest levels in the inner sanctum of UPP decision making. They 'came out a dat... and were allowed not only to 'come into dis' ... in some cases 'dem take over disya'!

How naïve is it for anyone to think that these scheming and conniving "Tent" usurpers, who had been living parasitically off our people under the other tent – who enlarged themselves there, would change after twenty-eight years of being addicted to 'million dollar' profiteering and free-wheeling, corruptive scamming of the people's resources?

Who in their right minds would think that these conspirators would change from their red stripes or switch their allegiances from the 'vultures' who they propped up for over a quarter of a century?

Who in the UPP made the decision to continue to keep the mongoose as guards outside the fowl house? And in many cases, some were even elevated to higher positions (inside the fowl house)! We will pay... and the UPP leaders who made those decisions – that short-sighted, grandiose, politically elementary decision - will pay for that lack of wisdom about mongoose behaviors.

Common sense should tell us that whatever they used to do... they are still doing... and probably more of it now. Whoever masters they used to serve... they are still serving! But... they are also now covered and protected under the **UPP Big Tent!**

Again, Yagyu Munenori's comment is insightful. "The consideration given to the **selection of officials** and the security of the nation is also an art of war."

So in that context, before it's too late, the UPP leadership needs to reconsider its *selection of officials* many of whom are still 'dyed in the red' **ALP** supporters boldly (not even covertly) strutting about under the **UPP's Big Tent.**

And, the UPP leadership needs to reconsider its selection of officials, who are 'supposedly' *former* 'dyed in red' members of the ALP structure (some quite high), and 'former' ALP financial supporters, who are now anointed (elected and appointed) princes of the UPP.

Again according to Yagyu Munenori, what is at stake in this war is nothing less than "the security of the nation."

If not the nation... then at least, the security of the **Government** in the **Sunshine** is at stake. And of course...

what is at stake is also the survival of the UPP as we know it today.

Take heed. Scrap the tent!

NEVER AGAIN

Saturday, October 22, 2005

For over a quarter century, many of us believed and hoped that our elected leaders represented our yearnings and desires, as well as our goals and objectives. But the truth was that the political leaders of those days represented their own yearnings and desires for money, property, social status, and the authority to direct others to do their bidding. They wanted these things for themselves - *first*... and somewhere down the road, at a much later date (if ever) - for the rest of us. Just like the leaders at Merck and Enron, our former political leaders made fabulous promises and commitments – particularly close to elections. After winning their constituencies, their commitments receded into the background as they began wrestling to fulfill their private personal agendas and desires. Year after year, they reneged on their commitments and betrayed the trust of their constituents.

And year after year, election after election, their constituents - the hopeful, trusting people of Antigua and Barbuda gave them another chance. And another. And another. And another... only to be disappointed, betrayed and fooled year after year. Again and again. Election after election.

While the elected filled their coffers, wielded their power, used and abused the innocent, parlayed public property for private gain, and courted international barons, immigrant profiteers, criminal privateers, and 'pirates of the Caribbean' – all of whom camouflaged themselves as neo-nationals.

Never again… should we allow any of our leaders, religious or secular, to betray our trusting people.

Never again, should we allow the scoundrels of the past to wield control over our domain again. Why not? Because they will do as they have done. They can do no different. They are who they are… true to themselves. A leopard and his spots?

True to themselves… A story clarifying this point is in order.

A story is told of a meeting between a frog and a scorpion. As the frog was about to swim across a stream, the scorpion approached and asked him for a ride. The frog said, "No! Do you think I am crazy? If I give you a ride on my back… I know what's going to happen. You are going to 'sting' me… and since your sting is posionous… I will die."

The scorpion replied that the frog was being stupid… because if he stung the frog while in the water… then both of them would die since he, the scorpion could not swim. He pleaded with the frog. He begged. He promised (just like a politician would). But the frog would not give him a ride. He got down on his knees. He told the frog that he did not want to die… He made such a powerful and persuasive argument that the frog relented and gave him a ride.

As they were going across… the scorpion stung the frog. As they were both dying… the frog from the poison… and the scorpion from being drowned… the frog asked the scorpion why he had done it. The scorpion replied… "I stung you because that's what scorpions do. We sting!"

Yep… that's what **some** politicians do. They betray trust. They are unethical. They look out for themselves. They are who they are. They cannot change. They will not change.

They see no reason to change. They have profited from their illegal profiteering. They form allegiances with international barons, immigrant privateers and 'pirates of the Caribbean' to disenfranchise the poor and innocent - and really all of us. They are like scorpions. Their sting is deadly to us. Unlike the scorpion ... they will survive to sting again and again and again... *if we let them.*

Yes... Those politicians who have stung us already... *will sting us again*... **if we let them.**

We won't. **Never again.** We will not go back.

Here is a warning to those who have not yet stung us... to those who promise sunshine and transparency.

Don't try 'to sting us'. It won't work. We are watching you closely. You should be aware that you are now under the new spotlight. Your own sunshine has enveloped you. Some of you are already close to the edge.... Some of you might already be over the edge... You have tasted the power. You may have seen the possibilities. You may be tempted. **Don't try it.**

The world of politics in Antigua and Barbuda has changed. The sun is shining through. The spotlight has been turned on. And, that light can never be turned off. Our people have slowly awakened. And we are demanding high ethics from your high offices. We are demanding transparency in decision making. We demand that no deals be made in the shadows... not among yourselves... not with any international baron or immigrant profiteer or privateer... and specifically not with the so-called 'nationalized' "pirate of the Caribbean". Money will not protect international barons, local privateers, immigrant profiteers or pirates from the wrath of those who have been stung... You will not be protected from the vengeance of the children of the victims.

Keep the sun shining in. Up with people. Down with *laborious* political parties of the past!

Never again will we return to the shallow, shadow, vulture-like politics of the past.

Never again.

The Voice of the People - *Part 1*

A fundamental change has occurred in Antigua and Barbuda. That change began over twenty years ago with the incisive, elegant, powerful and thought provoking writings of Tim Hector. His "Fan the Flame" is arguably the best series of socio/ political penmanship ever to grace the pages of a Caribbean newspaper (maybe any newspaper).

It is clear that Mr. Hector's "Fan the Flame" stirred deep yearnings in the populace for higher levels of ethical behavior, responsiveness and accountability among our leaders. His clear portrayals of corruption, shady dealings, self-serving (and family-serving) decisions by government leaders gave ordinary Antiguans and Barbudans their first glimpse into how public officials used their public office for private and personal gain.

The "Outlet" opened a window and 'let us in' to the dark workings of the government. And it continued to do so for decades.

In more recent times, however, for whatever reason, prior to his unfortunate passing, Mr. Hector seemed to have changed his outlook and his newspaper subsequently changed how it looked at the same government that for so many years he had soundly, roundly and unapologetically castigated.

While much of the reasoning for this flip flop is murky… one thing remains crystal clear: *The Outlet and Mr. Hector in his "Fan the Flame" provided a monumental service to Antiguans and Barbudans… and provided the impetus for the rise of another monumental contributor to the 'stirring of the deep yearnings' of the people of our nation.*

Where Mr. Hector's "Fan the Flame" started the yearnings, the Daily Observer and particularly the Observer Radio "Fanned the Bonfire".

While the Daily Observer continued the Outlet's tradition of revealing the hidden dealings of corruption in high places, it was the Observer Radio that allowed ordinary folk to respond and comment on the revelations.

That was new in Antigua and Barbuda.

Before, we had benefited from the precise, powerful and passionate thoughts and ideas of the university educated Tim Hector in his "Fan the Flame". But now we were hearing en masse, for the first time - the precise, powerful and passionate thoughts, ideas and feelings of the common folk, many of whom had not even gone as far as the seventh standard classes in the old colonial educational system. Many of the callers had waited that long to have a voice and to have their say in the affairs of their country.

With the advent of talk radio initiated by the Observer Radio, Antigua has changed. Undeniably so. Irrevocably so.

Now, I am not a historian, and some persons might lay claim that there was this or that radio talk show in Antigua prior to the Observer Radio. And they may be right. But no prior talk show program or its host can lay claim to having been the "Voice of the People."

The Voice of the People. And it was… and may still be the voice of the people. And yes… there are now other voices…

of and from the people. And that is as it should be. And there should be many more programs and hosts... because we need to hear from all of the people – all of the time - no matter their perspectives, persuasions or positions.

So Antigua and Barbuda has changed. The Voice of the People can now be heard in its many forms throughout the land, across the sea, on the internet and from far, far away.

Those of you who deal in the shadows... beware. The people are not only listening and watching... they are now talking – in public – and on the air!

Yes, Antigua and Barbuda has changed. And it is a change for the good.

THE VOICE OF THE PEOPLE - *PART 2*

Tuesday, November 15, 2005

With the coming of popular talk radio to the Antiguan and Barbudan airwaves, everyone could now have a say and expound philosophically on the practical matters that affected their nation, their community, their jobs, their households and their family.

And, no one can doubt that talk radio, specifically Winston Derricks' "The Voice of the People", was a 'monumental' player in the political developments of March 2004.

While people had read Tim Hector's "Fan the Flame", they could not respond, interact or 'have their say'. But with Observer Radio, they called in, they came in, and they emailed in. And when they didn't do any of those things, the station – from time to time - carried the microphone out into the streets so that all and sundry could have their say on "The Voice of the People".

So, Antigua and Barbuda has changed. Dramatically so. And it is a good thing.

People are not only reading and listening. Now they are verbally responding. And they now have alternative means (beyond Observer Radio) to let their voices be heard. They are hearing each other and dialoguing together – on all the sides of any issue.

And yes, it is a great thing that has happened. It might even be considered revolutionary. This is an occurrence that politicians in Antigua and Barbuda have taken note of and have started to utilize to serve their various agendas. And that is also a good thing.

This change has brought a measure of sunlight to our shores. Now, very little can be hidden from the people. Underhanded deals will be brought out to light. Corruption will be uncovered in days and weeks, rather than the years that it took prior to Observer Radio. Not only will it be uncovered early, it will be discussed by all and sundry before the week is out.

Old and new political leaders, and highly placed government officials no longer have the luxury of the anonymity of their actions. The sad thing is that while the old guard may have gotten the message (many of them are gone)... many of the new guard may have not. Some appear to want to roll back the clock to the days prior to "The Voice of the People" and probably prior to Tim Hector's "Fan the Flame".

Some of the new guard, the new elite leaders (elected, appointed & promoted) having benefited from the passionate contributions of the people's voices, are now wishing for these voices to be silent. Having benefited from the spotlight that was placed on the old guard, some of the new guard now wish to hide in the shadows and even draw the curtains to hide the sunshine.

But that will never happen again. Not in Antigua and Barbuda. The Flames have been Fanned into a Bonfire! They have spread the light across the land. And these flames cannot be dowsed.

Leaders across Antigua and Barbuda are now being held to a high standard – not by people like me with high degrees of education. They are particularly held to a high standard by the people of Antigua and Barbuda who have high degrees of common sense. By the people who now have the tools to articulate their high degrees of common sense.

Whether it is a 'doc-ies-ment' placed under a windshield wiper... or an anonymous live call to a call-in show... or an email to the 'Serpent'. The sting of public exposure will be the result.

And soon, we hope we can see videos of clandestine meetings and the behaviors of corrupt officials caught candidly on camera... aired and viewed on what maybe the *"People's Television".*

The "Voices of the People" cannot ever be silenced in Antigua and Barbuda... whether those voices are heard on Observer Radio or any other medium.

As my 91 year old mother likes to say... "A word to the wise ought to be sufficient!"

Antigua and Barbuda has changed.

And, it is a good thing.

ETHICAL CONDUCT AMONG PUBLIC OFFICIALS

Wednesday, December 21, 2005

According to a recent report in the Antigua Sun newspaper, Justice Don Mitchell QC said that, "Generations of Antiguans have lost all knowledge of what is the proper way to treat public assets and how to behave with the greatest propriety and what rules there are that should be followed; so that well-meaning people, people who mean best, simply don't know, simply don't understand what the correct procedures are."

Wow! Generations who had lost all knowledge... Generations of well-meaning people who simply don't know and simply don't understand how to behave... what rules there are... what rules should be followed... what correct procedures are?

Justice Mitchell reportedly said that over the years Antigua & Barbuda had become a case study "of the phenomenon where there's been a decline in the attention to integrity and good governance."

Over the last quarter century, Antigua and Barbuda had become a 'case study' in poor governance and the decline of integrity. A 'case' for the world to see, wonder and marvel at, evaluate, and... yes... 'study'!

Although he did not reveal the details of his findings (at least – I didn't see them), he did indicate that whatever he found during his investigation of public officials, "It was not because they are corrupt, but that they simply don't know any better."

Ha! I don't agree that these people – public sector officials – leaders who presented themselves as all-powerful and all-knowledgeable – could now be allowed an excuse… "We didn't know any better!" No… I don't buy that.

The decline of integrity, increases in impropriety, exhibition of poor governance, questions about corruption, not knowing how to treat public assets – these are all symptoms of very low levels of ethical conduct among public officials.

The management of ethics in public office is an essential part of good governance. It is a way to ensure the credibility of any public administration which may suffer from a lack of public respect and which may be criticized for a paucity of honesty, integrity and impartiality. Such seems to have been the case in Antigua and Barbuda during the long tenure of the previous administration.

The United Progressive Party (UPP), in its 2004 Manifesto seem to have recognized the need for ethics in public office in its assertion that *"**Integrity will be the bedrock of the UPP**"* if they were elected. Surely, the UPP recognized (as have many other commonwealth governments around the world) that without a Code of Ethics which is vigorously enacted, monitored and faithfully employed, there is the potential for a "weakening of the moral compass of ministers and civil servants, a greater willingness to contemplate actions which are improper, and an unhealthy closeness between ministers and civil servants" to the detriment of the country's citizens.

Many Antiguans and Barbudans would undoubtedly agree that such 'weakening of the moral compass of ministers and civil servants' might have been demonstrated in March, 2004 with the reportedly clandestine removal of files from various ministries by public officials – purportedly at the behest of their former ministerial superiors.

Furthermore, during the last quarter century, hundreds of allegations were directed against public officials that seem to have indicated that some public servants had an increasingly 'greater willingness to contemplate actions that were improper'. However, I hasten to add that many of these allegations highlighted in various media **presumed** not *contemplation* of improper actions... but **assumed** that 'improper actions' were actually carried out at the ministerial level and at all grades and ranks of public officials.

It has also been suggested that in such situations as existed over the last quarter century here in Antigua and Barbuda, that some government leaders seem to have treated the Civil Service like its 'fiefdom'. According to one theorist, when a government emanates a strong scent, the Civil Service is likely to pick it up. Some are repelled by it, some attracted to it. As a consequence, the Civil Service becomes highly politicized. This was the case... is the case... in Antigua and Barbuda. It is still the case today because many of the Civil Servants who seemed to have identified themselves with the former administration's 'fiefdom' appear not to have relinquished that identity. They continue to act in ways that question their integrity and impartiality as it relates to the carrying out of their duties as Civil Servants and public officials.

Adding to the confusion on this issue is the tenet that "Civil Servants should fully serve the Government of the day." While it is clear that Civil Servants should fully carry out the dictates and mandates of the Government of day, it should also be noted that Civil Servants cannot do so in contravention of other legal, ethical or professional precepts or requirements. In other words, Civil Servants have an obligation to give honest and faithful service, to act in a manner consistent with the bond of trust and confidence of the citizenry, to act impartiality and with integrity, and to obey the law.

Even more importantly, ethical behavior applies to Ministers of Government and top public officials. For example, the code of conduct of one commonwealth government, states that, "Ministers have a duty to refrain from asking or instructing civil servants to do things which they should not do." They also have a duty to ensure that Civil Servants are not asked to engage in activities likely to call in question their 'political impartiality', or to give rise to the criticism that public funds are being used for party or political purposes."

When one attends to the very loud public discourse in the media, it is clear that issues such as maladministration, corruption, lack of integrity and impropriety in public office are increasingly areas of deep concern to the citizens of Antigua and Barbuda.

With the foregoing in mind, and with full awareness that the UPP Government has made a commitment to increase the levels of integrity, transparency and accountability in public administration, it seems that it is time to place a higher level of focus and sustained attention to improving the ethical and professional behaviors of public officials of all grades and ranks in Antigua and Barbuda.

Antigua and Barbuda cannot continue to be "a case study of the *phenomenon* where there's been a decline in the attention to integrity and good governance." We cannot accept that, "It was not because they are corrupt, but that they *simply don't know any better*." We will not accept it from Ministers of Government and other elected officials, Senators, Consultants, Advisors, Statutory Board Members, Permanent Secretaries or any other public official.

I must address Justice Mitchell's statement that "it wasn't because they are corrupt', and that these highly placed, highly qualified officials 'simply don't know any better.' His assertions stretches my imagination to its very limits... and I still find it hard to accept... that they 'simply don't know any better'. But, we may not ever be able to prove that some officials, in recent or past history, acted and behaved consciously, willingly, purposefully and with full intent.

So, we must first accept that they can and must do better.

Secondly, we must ensure that future generations of Antiguan and Barbudan public officials regain and then retain the knowledge *and practice* of propriety, integrity and honesty in the pursuance of their obligations as 'Civil' *servants*!

Thirdly, we must put the mechanisms in place to hold public officials fully accountable for unethical conduct. Such mechanisms must have sanctions as sharp as shark teeth. And those who monitor their behaviors must be vigilant and demonstrate their willingness to apply the sanctions.

Generations of Antiguans and Barbudans will greatly appreciate that our twin island state would have moved from the current disgraceful status to become a 'case study' in excellent governance, with demonstrated high levels of propriety and integrity!

CONFLICT OF INTEREST IN HIGH OFFICE?

Wednesday, December 07, 2005

According to the online version of an Antiguan Newspaper (December 7th, 2005), an opposition Member of Parliament, launched a 'fiery attack' on the family of a prominent businessman. This attack came during the debate on the 2006 budget. According to the newspaper, the opposition MP charged that there was a *blatant conflict of interest* for government to elevate a businessman to senior political office *while his business is still doing business with the government.*

That reported charge by the opposition member of parliament gave me great pause. It does not matter what I think of the member of parliament and his political exploits or activities in the past. It does not matter what I think of the MP and his current political woes with his own party. It does not matter what I think of the man personally whatever the rumors or loud whispers.

His charge that there is a *blatant conflict of interest for government to elevate a businessman to senior political office* **while** *his business is still doing business with the government* is **at least** worthy of some thought.

Over the last quarter century, the former Antigua Labour Party (ALP) Administration, was constantly bombarded with charges of corruption and unethical 'wheelings and dealings'. (Indeed, if I remember correctly, the opposition MP himself was at the center of some of these charges – though unsubstantiated – at least up until this point.)

Over those years, the United Progressive Party (UPP) was front and center along with the media in challenging the ALP Government on each and every questionable deal that came to light. They took a principled and ethical stance against corruption in high office, against wheelings and dealings, and indeed... against any negotiations or agreements that, to them, had the **appearance** of illegality or impropriety.

Now that the UPP forms the Government, much is expected of them... not the least of which is that they embrace the same principled and ethical stances that they so ardently and passionately represented in their very public criticisms of the then ALP Government.

Much is expected of them... to avoid not only wrong doing... but the **appearance** of illegality and impropriety in **their** high offices.

I would argue, then, that we look carefully at the opposition MP's posturing in the House – whether it represented a personal vendetta against the family of the elevated businessman... whether it represented a political vendetta, or whether it represented the ruminations of a man who had finally been touched by Grace.

Whatever it represented, that reported statement there is a *blatant conflict of interest for government to elevate a businessman to senior political office while his business is still doing business with the government* needs to be seriously examined.

The following questions do not presume or assume that conflicts exist. They are offered not only to examine the potential for conflict... but as *preventative warnings* of what could happen in the future… whether its with this official (the elevated business man) or some other.

Questions need to be asked… and answered.

- Does the elevated businessman recluse himself from Cabinet discussions on matters that impact the various business sectors in which his companies are involved?

- More to the point… Does the businessman recluse himself… or is he asked to recluse himself from discussions having to do with APUA and electricity generation, importation of cars (new or used), import taxes for businesses, etc?

- Within the context of Cabinet decision-making, is the elevated businessman allowed to vote on, or discuss, or influence decisions on matters that impact his business interests?

- Does the businessman (an Antiguan citizen – *not by birth*) advise the members of Cabinet on matters that impact their decisions on matters pertinent to his business interests?

- Even as we examine this individual, we should also ask the same questions of some of the elected politicians who sit in Cabinet. Have they identified, revealed and 'fessed up' about their business investments, business holdings and formal business interests? These questions are not just about one individual – they apply to all who purport to be taking care of the people's business!

Please remember, that as a member of Cabinet – and indeed, both the Parliament and the Senate, the businessman (elevated as a reward?) is imbued with extraordinary influence. And remember, it is an influence that appears to be strong on both sides of the political aisle. This influence, in these contexts, as extraordinary as it is, must serve not his family business interests, but the interests of the Antiguan and Barbudan electorate.

Electorate? There-in and here-in lies the rub… he is not an elected official… he is an appointed official. He was not elevated to high office by the people for the enhancement of their interests. He was elevated – no rewarded – by the political directorate of the UPP. Of course, it is my belief that the UPP Directorate felt that they could benefit from his vast business experience.

But they ought to have instituted some rules and regulations governing the mechanics of his contributions while in such high office.

What are some of those rules? Here are at least two:

1. That he (and other cabinet officials who have similar interests and investments) should recluse himself from discussions on matters that impact the business sectors in which his companies are involved – including matters dealing with APUA.

2. That, within Cabinet, he should not vote on such matters when decisions were being made. (And indeed, he should take a principled stance not to discuss or vote on such matters in either Parliament or the Senate.)

I keep wondering what great benefit might the UPP Directorate have seen or expected in elevating the businessman to such high offices – particularly given his former alliances with the former administration? Did they need his advice and 'wise' counsel on matters in which he is an expert? Could they not have offered him a more focused role in an advisory capacity? Or was his elevation due to something else... maybe... like rewarding him for his financial, consulting or other contribution during the phases of the last election... maybe? Or both? Maybe not.

Let me be quick to say, that one need not question, analyze, demean or even try to understand the businessman's motivation to seek or accept the offer to serve in high official positions. That is not the question. Which business person would not seek such influence? There are many... many so-called supporters and hangers-on who have sought and won their political pieces-of-eight! No... we ought not to question his motives for seeking or accepting such appointments. Nor, should anyone try to cast any dispersion on his acceptance of the positions... It is his right to do so.

It is not the rewarded and then elevated businessman who we should question. It is his appointers and his upp-lifters whom we must ask questions of.

The question is this: Does his presence in Cabinet and in the halls of government reflect a position of undue influence where he could impact the decisions that are made at the highest levels of Government in our nation... specifically with regard to the decisions that impact the businesses in which he is involved?

Even if he has made no efforts to do so, should he be placed in a position where his very presence might represent a conflict of interest or where he himself may be conflicted in his decision-making capacity?

Here is another question: Does his presence in Cabinet give him an unfair advantage over his business competitors who are not privy to the detailed discussions on business issues (or opportunities) which could seriously impact them?

If the answers are yes... then we must bear in mind that such influence can be seen and interpreted, and have the **appearance** of, and does carry the real possibility of being, according to the opposition MP, "**A conflict of interest**" for a businessman elevated to "senior political office" **while** he has... not one – but several of his businesses which are *currently* "doing business" *with the same government that he is an integral part of.*

In my view, not only does this jaundice the whole relationship with the government (of which he is currently a part), but it could and would most likely seriously damage the government's credibility with both large and small business owners.

Furthermore, if it is perceived that he utilizes the advantageous position of his "senior political office", this could undermine and dampen the willingness of local and foreign entrepreneurs who want to invest in Antigua & Barbuda in those particular areas of business in which his companies participate and may be perceived to hold an unfair, unethical and unseemly advantage.

By the way, aren't issues of impropriety and conflict of interest the crux of the charges that are reportedly being examined in order to be put before the court against some individuals who held "senior political office" within the former administration?

A Brief History of Pirates & Privateers in the Caribbean - *Part I*

The history of piracy dates back more than 3000 years. Piracy was described in Homer's The Iliad and The Odyssey. It appears that the word pirate (peirato) was also used about 140 BC by the Roman historian Polybius. The Greek historian Plutarch, writing in about 100 A.D., gave a clear definition of piracy. He described pirates as those who attack without legal authority, not only ships, but also maritime cities.

In more modern times, particularly in the Caribbean Region, pirates operated with impunity. The names of Morgan the Pirate, Captain Kidd and Edward Teach – more infamously known as Blackbeard, struck terror in the hearts of ships' crews. In fact many of these pirates claimed a new name: "privateers". The difference apparently was that a privateer was a pirate who had a commission or letter from a government authorizing him to seize or destroy a vessel of another nation. Global powers such as England, France and Spain commissioned their 'private pirates' to prey on each others ships and 'New World' territories.

Sir Francis Drake was the first of the well known "privateers". Historically, he is considered a hero by the British but the Spanish consider him to have been a cruel and bloodthirsty pirate. Morgan the Pirate was also Sir Henry Morgan – having been recognized by the British Government for his exploits. He was later installed as Lieutenant Governor of Jamaica.

It is also noteworthy that privateers not only attacked ships, but also sacked and pillaged harbors, ports and seaside towns.

The exploits of these pirates, privateers or buccaneers as they were also known, is well depicted in the well known classic Treasure Island.

Today, unfortunately, we still have pirates and privateers plying their trade around the Caribbean Region. However, although these 'modern' day swashbuckling buccaneers still hunt for other people's gold and silver, they do so using modern piratical means such as money-trafficking, money cycling and other types of financial crimes. Again, quite regrettably, this Region is embraced by some modern day 'private pirates' of the Caribbean as a "haven" for their swashbuckling activities.

MODERN DAY PIRATES & PRIVATEERS IN THE CARIBBEAN - *PART 2*

Saturday, December 03, 2005

The modern day pirates and privateers of the Caribbean conduct their operations not from the sea, not from boats (maybe yachts) but from their private jets, continental main offices and local satellite offices.

Like pirates of old, these modern day prototypes of Morgan the Pirate and Blackbeard flaunt their money in grand style. Just like in days of old, they use their spoils to win the allegiance of the locals who live in these territories. They buy and then control the local and regional officialdom. They also use 'pieces of silver' to buy their way into the psyche of the people by propping up governments, and extravagantly funding sporting programs, political parties and community projects. They use money like drug pushers use cocaine… getting their victims addicted to the money and then using, abusing and then discarding them.

Like days of old, these modern day swashbuckling buccaneers in the Caribbean find this region such a 'haven', that they build their heavily fortified hideouts here. In the past, such hideouts were characterized by moats such that they were difficult to approach. Of course, these days, they build their lairs on small islands, protected by sophisticated underground (and undersea) high tech surveillance early warning systems. They are also protected by highly paid mercenaries who, like the buccaneers of old, are heavily armed, not with swords, knives and gun powder, but with... 'modern day' automatic gun power.

Some of these modern day pirates may also lay claim to the name "privateer" as did Morgan the Pirate and his ilk. They consort with the powerbrokers (senators & congress men) from today's global powers. Indeed, one wonders if some of their activities are not "sanctioned" by these powerbrokers who may turn an official "blind eye" to the highly questionable source of the flaunted wealth of these modern day pirates or privateers in the Caribbean.

Recent revelations in the halls of power in at least one of these global powers, indicate that some of these powerbrokers might themselves be quite susceptible to being addicted to the financial 'fixes' of the 'privateering pirates' in the Caribbean.

Indeed, the term privateer is not far fetched, since our modern day pirates also claim to be "private" international businessmen. One can imagine Sir Francis Drake or Captain Kidd claiming to be private businessmen with 'financial interests' in various 'ports and harbors' around the world.

Another similarity is striking. Today's pirates, turned privateers, like the buccaneers of days of old, find coves, hidden beaches, and small islands very attractive.

There is one other noteworthy similarity. Pirates and privateers are only attracted to territories that are associated with treasure.

One wonders then… to the extent that we may have such privateers buccaneering in Antiguan waters… what treasures might they know of that we don't?

Are the sunshine islands of Antigua & Barbuda "Treasure Islands"?

Stand Your Ground!

As we move deeper into the New Year, the critics of the Baldwin Spencer administration are gearing up for a concerted onslaught. Not only are the critics lining up to attack, other individuals have come together to form "spheres of influence" to pressure and manipulate the Government to adopt their agenda of financial gluttony.

My message to the Prime Minister is this:

Stand Your Ground
The wolves in sheep clothing have gathered around
Don't Back Down
Stand Firm on Your Ground...

It is understandable that an opposition party will critique and criticize. It is understandable that opposition party members will "oppose" the policies of the government of the day. Now everyone knows... that the core members of this opposition could any day now be charged with serious crimes of gross gluttonousness and excessively greedy, criminal corruption while they were in public office. We know this. And they know this. We know that they are guilty. And they know that they are guilty. What is beyond my understanding is the crass boldness of these gluttonous thieves. Men who gave themselves the Peoples' prime land for pennies and resold the same land not for pounds but for thousands of pounds... Men who received bribes from Piratical Privateers who operate in Antigua... now use those ill-gotten dollars to enrich themselves and masquerade as successful property owners and businessmen.

If these are the caliber of political opponents who critique and criticize the current government… then I say to the Cabinet….

Stand Your Ground…. Don't Back Down!

Even more distressing than these tainted political opponents, are those who claim to want to support the new administration and have formed blocks and spheres of influence so that they can "capitalize" on the treasure trove of opportunities that they perceive to exist. These opportunists include Privateers of American and Middle Eastern origins and operatives with local business interests.

These are the ones who pose the most danger to the Baldwin Spencer administration. There are several reasons for this. First, there seems to be a vacuum of knowledge and experience within the administration in many critical areas of governance. Indeed, for the first several months, the new government fumbled around because of this apparent lack, because of the lack of files and clear paper trail (thanks to the corrupt politicians of the former administration), and because of poor preparation in the years leading up to the UPP's success at the polls. Whatever the reasons for the vacuum of knowledge and experience, "supporters" appeared out of every 'nook and cranny' to "help" the new government.

Some of these 'experienced and knowledgeable' "supporters" had, of course, obtained their 'experience and knowledge' at the feet of, and in bed with, the 'corrupt politicians' of the last administration. Many of them had 'wheeled', 'dealed' and dined with the corrupt in high places. Many of them, leading up to the elections, had played both sides of the fence… hedging their bets… just in case. When the UPP won, they were in the right place, at the right time, with the right balance of capital, information and, of course, influence.

Now they seem to have the Baldwin Spencer administration in the palm of their gluttonous paws. Most of them sit in high places... officially and unofficially.

My message to the government is this...

For twenty plus years you formed a band
A tight 'brotherhood' to protect this, our land
Remember the lonely times when the 'brotherhood' fought together
Remember when you all but cried in despair on each other's shoulder

Don't let those privateering usurpers break that bond...
Don't let money and influence destroy your historical union
Remember that your "nabel 'tring" buried ya-so-so in this land...
Stand firm together with the 'brotherhood' and the people that elevated you to this position

The Baldwin Spencer administration swept into power with high promises of transparency, integrity and responsible fiscal policies. It is clear to me that they are valiantly attempting to hold fast to their promises. But, because of the wily dealings of the influential opportunists, the unity of the party behind the government, is beginning to crack. Many of these opportunists publicly give lip service to the principle of integrity, but privately, they say that now is *their* time. They claim they have suffered in exclusion for 28 years... and now they intend to reap the benefits of inclusion. And *they* pose a very serious threat to this government... because they can easily become the equivalent of those crassly bold, gluttonously greedy members and associates of the former administration...

Mr. Spencer....

Stand Your Ground
The wolves in sheep clothing
And the sheep in wolves clothing... have gathered around
Don't Back Down
Stand Firm *in* Your Ground!

BEWARE OF BLUNDERS

Thursday, February 16, 2006

I have been reading a series of books and articles on marketing and have been intrigued by the types of serious blunders that major corporations and organizations make. Many of these blunders are so costly that sometimes even the CEO gets fired!

As I examined some of these blunders, I thought of our twin island state, our new government, the new 'directors' and our new 'CEO'. I wondered at some of the blunders that our leaders 'might' be making and the potential cost if they don't do better.

Here a few of those costly blunders from the corporate world. I leave it to you the reader to apply them to issues and concerns you may have with our 'Sunshine Government'. (In some instances, I give in to the temptation to add a few artistic comments...)

Attempt "Business As Usual"

When a company has serious problems like issues with cash flow and charges of corruption and unethical practices, the leaders cannot act as if it is "business as usual". It won't be. When a company misses Wall Street expectations, institutes layoffs or closings, or announces some other bad news, it needs to rebuild lost confidence. Your brand has been damaged. Your shareholders and stakeholders (supporters and voters?) will look at you with a more critical eye. People will doubt you in ways they never used to. It will take time to rebuild. Rather than "business as usual", act as if it is "business unusual". Get busy. Communicate. Be transparent. Take massive and continuous action. And, keep your promises!

Lie, Mislead, and otherwise Obfuscate

Lying never works. It sounds obvious, but companies and executives (and politicians?) do it all the time. It can land you in jail or ruin your career (well – we have yet to see that in Antigua & Barbuda). People hate delivering bad news, so they tell a "white lie" which they often rationalize as somehow doing good for others. Or, some people don't tell the whole truth. They only state the minimum they have to.

Be honest and direct about the facts. Be *brutally honest* about the facts… and stop putting all the blame on your predecessors. If they did something wrong then your shareholders or stakeholders will take action (they already did… they put you in charge!)

Start by being honest with yourself about the condition of the business (and the country) and your role in what has happened or is happening. Get clear about this. Then you can decide how best to handle the situation.

Be honest with your stakeholders and shareholders (voters and supporters). If you are laying 25% of your people off, then say that's what you are doing. Don't say, "We are laying off 15% and expect some additional headcount reductions through normal attrition." Don't say we want 700 staff members to take the package *if* you really want 1500 to do so!

Not Communicating…

The truth will never be as bad as the rumors will become. "No comment" or worse… not communicating with the public will increase the untruths and gossip. It will also unleash the venom of the people you used to be forthright with. The press will attack harder, and your employees' and your stakeholders' distrust and mistrust will grow deeper. People will begin to make comparisons with the worst past experiences that they have had. This will undermine your efforts with customers and stakeholders and drive your 'stock' down. It doesn't matter how much it hurts. You must over communicate – particularly if you have a history of effective communicating 'in the past'.

Don't be surprised if the press and analysts misquote you, or only use part of what you said to make you or your company (or government) look worse. It happens. Get over it. That comes with the job of being a senior executive (minister?). The bottom line is, if you don't explain the condition the business or economy is in and what you are doing about it, things will get much worse.

Communicate Confusing Messages

When you're in trouble, get clear about what you are going to say before you open your mouth. Rambling or trying to make 16 points will make you look confused, defensive, or stupid.

Appoint no more than three executives to do the talking: your CEO and two others. Then get clear on three -- and only three – key messages for them to deliver: the facts as you know them, the actions you're taking now, and how your actions today, position you for future success. Write these messages down, and practice saying them. Get a speech coach! Get a speech coach!

Write down every possible question you can anticipate from customers, employees, partners, shareholders, press, and analysts. Underneath each, write the number of one of the key messages that best answers the question. Practice answering those questions with a key message until you can recite them in your sleep. Then practice them again. All three people should be saying the same thing. No diversions. No ad libbing. No 'un-rehearsed' off-the-cuff remarks. (Yes... you have that right! All spontaneous, off-the-cuff remarks should be rehearsed!!!)

And, oh yes! Speaking on the platform is different from speaking in the boardroom. The CEO should get a speech coach! But speak in your voice and with your passion!

Believe Confidential and Internal Communications Are Internal and Confidential!

Write every email as if it will be printed in the morning newspaper and posted on the Internet. It will be. Do the same thing with your regular mails and conversations.

Don't kid yourself about this. It doesn't matter how much you trust the people you are working with. Someone *absolutely* will leak the information. Particularly when you least expect it. Assume that all of your stakeholders *and* competitors will be on every internal video or audio conference-call. Assume that whenever you speak, wherever you speak, to whomever you speak, that there is a "Voice" listening. "Steel" yourself and get ready for the "Fire" of criticisms that will come your way because of what you said. Or, don't say it!

Understand that your executive management, board of directors, auditors, lawyers, consultants, (cabinet, party members, constituents, inner-circle members) and friends will leak information. No matter how much they promise not to. No matter how many confidentiality agreements they sign.

Forget this, and you'll get stung. Hard!

Play Defense

Within three weeks of your bad-news announcement, you must launch a strong marketing offense. Why three weeks? First, people need time to digest the bad news and recover from what happened. Second, if you wait much longer, your stakeholders (supporters and voters) will assume that you have no future and will start bailing on you. And your competition will be holding a wake (with wine, champagne and Cavalier)

Launch an integrated marketing offensive targeted at customers, prospects, partners, shareholders, stakeholders, employees, and 'competitors' about the future of your business (government & party). It should include: three keys to the turnaround, a vision for the future of your 'industry' (party), and a vision for the future of your business as an industry leader.

The CEO – not the economists, not the lawyers, not the chief financial officer – must demonstrate the leader's vision for the future of the enterprise!

THE WRITING ON THE WALL: *STOP PLANNING & START DOING*

Friday, February 17, 2006

I have taken it upon myself to read, re-read and read again the writings of one of Antigua's giants of history, economy and philosophy: Tim Hector.

As much as I have been dumfounded by the political company he kept in his later years, this pales in comparison to the awe in which I hold the man for his insight, clarity in articulation and depth of perspective.

And so, I would like to share with you a few paragraphs from a 1996 "Fan the Flame" Article entitled: "Lester Bird Broke the Neck of the Economy".

"It is not an accident that the 'best and brightest' in Antigua over the last twenty years did not go into the productive and creative sectors. They went into traditional professions, law, medicine, and teaching. Few went into management, engineering, or marketing. This was because the productive sectors of the Antigua and Barbuda economy became even more underdeveloped between 1976 and 1996.

We are going to suffer in the future from this lack of trained personnel for modern industrial and productive activity. Besides, the free movement of skilled labour in all CARICOM territories, is going to make Antigua & Barbuda a net importer of skilled labour. This together with the fact, that nearly one-third of the Antigua labour force some 7,300 workers are already 'foreign nationals' will complicate both politics and economics here. The economy is a thorough-going Bird mess."

Imagine that Tim Hector in 1996 was predicting that we would suffer from the "lack of trained personnel for modern industrial and productive activity." Listen to the nurses at Holberton, have a discussion with a police officer, call your child's teacher, talk with your mechanic… the chances are that you would be speaking with someone from either Cuba, Guyana, Jamaica, St. Vincent… and well… even Dominica! And if you speak with a business owner in English Harbour, Redcliffe Key or a real estate agent from addresses unknown – you will be speaking with someone from Wisconsin, Texas, Singapore, Germany, Canada or some such place!

Furthermore, Tim Hector saw what would happen with the advent of CSME! *"The free movement of skilled labor… will make Antigua and Barbuda a net importer of skilled labour."* All because our political leaders failed to encourage, motivate and stimulate young Antiguans and Barbudans to go into the *'productive and creative'* sectors! And, it is my contention that the threat from Caribbean Nationals pales in comparison to the future hegemonic threat from the neo-colonialists (economic pirates and privateers) from North America and Europe. (But that is another discussion for another article.)

Tim Hector continues: *"Simultaneously, Antigua and Barbuda, under successive Bird administrations did nothing to develop its human resources: from management through entry level labourers. That is, did nothing to train managers and provide labourers with skills. There was no plan. Therefore, those things dignified with the name "skills training" were pork-barrel patronage programmes, to provide workers to existing firms, with the government paying millions of dollars went down the drain. These millions added to the disastrous assembly type foray, made awful financial matters worse. No project instituted under* *the aegis of Lester Bird has ever worked. Each and everyone has always been a drain on the national treasury."*

Not only did millions of dollars go down the drain... so did the talents and aspirations of thousands of children in primary and secondary schools. They looked around and they saw few opportunities for a robust economic future. They looked around and saw their mothers and fathers, uncles and aunts going to dead end jobs, learning nothing new and doing nothing creative, sitting at desks twiddling their thumbs, passing ledgers from one desk to another... under productive and underperforming...

These same children had a window to the world through CNN, MTV, Cartoon Network and Nickelodeon. They kind of knew that it was different elsewhere... that there was a mismatch between what was happening in Antigua and Barbuda... and the rest of the world - and even the rest of the Caribbean.

These children watched as they moved from Infant 1 to Junior 5... and noticed that their teachers were changing... that the doctors in the clinics were changing... that the nurses at the hospital were changing... These children watched as successive governments were unable or unwilling to find an Antiguan or Barbudan who could serve as Attorney General. When they went to the National Museum, they found a non-Antiguan/Barbudan telling them about our history. All around them, their uncles, aunts, and cousins had been marginalized and in some ways made irrelevant to the national scheme of things. And somewhere in the inner consciousness they knew that their future chances were limited... their birthrights were being stolen right from under them... their futures were dim... and they knew and know it. Go to any school... Ottos, Bendals, Golden Grove, Pigotts... look into their eyes... I can tell you... these are not the eyes that I saw when I taught in 1978. No they are not.

I am from Perry Bay... Tinning Village... Grays Farm. I taught at Greenbay School. Each time I pass through the area... I see the children of students that I taught... hanging on the corners. I even see their parents hanging on the same corners. Unemployed. Underemployed. And some... well... unaccustomed to employment.

And, each time I pass... or walk by... someone looks up through eyes dimmed with pain and disillusionment and shouts, "Mr. Mottley!" Or, "Teacher!" And, tears come to my heart and find a path to my eyes.

Anyone who dismisses the quarter century of "Birdonomics" as just another set of chapters in our history, have not really walked through Grays Farm, Point, or Old Road with their eyes open. They like some of my former students have been numbed and drugged by years of abandonment by the political elite, or they were blinded by their own marginal successes.

Tim Hector in his 1996 article, called for the then Bird government to change the way they did business. As pre-requisites to any success, he called for *"an accountable government, free of scandal, which can mobilize the public for the economic tasks at hand. Nothing else will do. The more we wait, the worse it will become. Time is against us. A scandal-ridden regime, **cannot**, repeat, cannot, mobilize any nation, anywhere, anytime. Need I say more? The economic writing is on the wall, for all to see and read. Those who will not hear, the old adage goes, will feel. Nothing educates like feeling."*

"The economic writing is on the wall." Today, February 17th, 2006, fully ten years after Hector wrote his article, we have a new administration. Yet, it is not clear to me that we (or they) have been fully educated by the failures of the past.

My heart is still crying not only for the plight of my former students, but for the condition that their children and grandchildren find themselves in.

I am yet to see any changes in Greenbay, Grays Farm, Point or Old Road or even to get the feeling that substantive changes are on the way. I am yet to see any changes in those communities that would give me a sense of hopefulness and motivation.

We have changed our leaders… but have we changed the way we do things?

I believe that some of our new leaders have the right intentions… but they surround themselves with people whose intentions are at least questionable. A business person who is disconnected from our community… who has never been connected to our community… who is your advisor… confidante and constant companion… will not be reminding you of the plight of your people.

His conversations will not be about training the kids of the Jarvis', the Davis' or the Brown's. He will be talking about relaxing the laws so that he can import this or that from China or Brazil. He will not be whispering about fixing the housing situation along Christian Street or Armstrong Road or doing anything about Perry's Bay and 'Tinning Village'. Instead, he will be trying to get his hands on the exclusive no-bid contract to build the next government office, or grab that prime piece of land for next to nothing for some 'will-o-wisp' project that will bring him and his family millions more in dollars.

I am yet to see training for the people who need it in areas where they can feel a sense of pride and contribution, a sense of belonging and ownership - and a sense that they can make a real living.

I see even more foreign nurses, teachers, mechanics and police officers – not to mention accountants, lawyers, attorneys general... even unelected ministers of government! Now we even have Chinese auto mechanics... Chinese supermarket owners... Chinese construction companies... and too many of those Chinese 'greasy spoon' restaurants have become the food-shop of choice for our people. Soon we will have Chinese fishermen, Chinese farmers... and who knows what else.

I am yet to see a major initiative to address the plight of indigenous Antiguans and Barbudans, to increase their skill levels, enhance their professional training and qualifications so that they can raise themselves out of the quagmire (mud) in which they were abandoned by the former and seemingly ignored by the current.

Two years pales in comparison to twenty-eight years of scandalous abandonment. Yes. But... two years is still too long. We cannot wait for the economy to be right. We cannot wait for the deficit to be reduced. We cannot wait to weigh the options. We cannot wait for the consultations. We cannot wait for the programmes to move from the drawing board to the planning board. We have waited for over a quarter century. We can wait no longer! We have been planning what we would do... ought to do when the time came.

Enough of this action planning. Stop planning and start taking action!

"The economic writing is on the wall." The social writing is in our face. We need real change, real fast!

PIRATES IN HEROES CLOTHING

Monday, June 12, 2006

Why are we surprised that our resident Pirate of the Caribbean is heartless? A quote from Kurt Vonnegut should give us both insight and clarity about our modern day "**Pirate in Heroes Clothing.**"

"The chief weapon of pirates, was their capacity to astonish. Nobody else could believe, until it was too late, how heartless and greedy they were."

Certainly, over the last ten years, Antiguans and Barbudans have been *astonished* by the nefarious, malicious, vengeful, controlling, and manipulative ploys of the Pirate of the Caribbean who partially resides here.

"*Nobody could believe*" it when the pilots were threatened, when the islands were filched, when the airport lands were purloined, when credible Antiguans were incredibly enticed into and then unceremoniously kicked out from his organization, when... well, it's too much... let me stop.

But I must add that many people who sincerely believed that this "Pirate" was a "Hero" are now doing an abrupt 'about face' in light of his recent *heartless* action related to a local program involving a "House" full of dependent women and children.

The fact is that Vonnegut is right... Pirates, whether they are from the Caribbean or elsewhere are not only 'heartless' they are also *greedy... excessively greedy*. Modern day pirates like the one who has leeched himself onto us, will not be involved in anything unless there is either an obvious or devious and carefully manipulated scheme behind their apparently "*heroic*" offerings.

Pirates will offer you a carrot and when it is time to spring their trap, they will of course snatch it away. The bigger the carrot... the more devious the trap. And there is something else... the bigger the victim's perceived need... the bigger the carrot and the more devious, elaborate and emotionally appealing the trap will be.

These are not ordinary carrots. Pirates, we must remember, deal only in gold and silver and things that are precious and of high value. And their gold and silver don't belong to them either... they 'acquire' those from other people. So these are 'acquired' golden carrots that are offered to needy victims.

And we in Antigua are ripe for the pickings... vulnerable because there is a lot of need... just the kind of situation for a greedy pirate. Pirates of old never operated in England, or their home territories. Modern day pirates don't operate their piratical activities in their homes either... There, they are on their best behavior... Apparently... But here... we are easy pickings - psychologically and materially!

A case in point is our needy cricketing teams not only from Antigua... but from around the region – and of course our Windies cricket team. Their needs are off the charts...

So here comes the Pirate of... well... the West Indies... Here he comes with a humongous golden carrot... wait... not one carrot... but a whole 'crocus bag' full of them... And of course, our cricket legends get sucked in, our cricket boards get sucked in, (the politicians are already sucked in), our cricketers get sucked in... and of course the public gets sucked in... into the trap of course.

When will the trap be sprung? Who knows? The pirate of course... He knows... it's part of his elaborate plan...

There is a psychological, Machiavellian one-man game going on. It is a simple ruse. It is also a psycho-physiological ploy used by the drug cartels (that is an intriguing parallel). Get the people hooked... and you have got them addicted and dependent for life! In this case, money is the drug...

Forget about teaching people to fish... just give them the fish... make them dependent... and you can take their lands, their houses, their little islands, corrupt their best minds, make the best and brightest of their youth dependent on and addicted to their 'gold', control their political parties, manipulate their politicians, own their ministers (both types)... take away their big island, own and manipulate the current "king's" advisors, maybe even one day - own the "king"... or become the "king".

Sounds impossible? Well if you analyze the above carefully, our resident Pirate is more than half way there...

Let's go back to Vonnegut's quotation: *"The chief weapon of pirates was their capacity to astonish. Nobody else could believe, until it was too late, how heartless and greedy they were."*

Let us focus on the phrase *"until it was too late."* It's too late for those pilots. It's too late for .... - (well I don't want to call my friend's name), it's too late for some of the staff bribed, enticed and stolen away from our indigenous airline (then, of course, kicked to the curb) ... it's too late for the contractors that were sacked... it's too late to get our lands back... it's too late to get our islands back… and the Airport… well – that's an on-going story.

And it is too late for the poor, unfortunate residents of the House…. All they wanted was the temporary shelter they were promised, a hot meal and somewhere to lay their heads at night. That's all they wanted… temporary relief! But…

It will soon be too late for LIAT – that's another story for a different article.

It might take one year, or it might take five… (it took 8 years before the heroic plans for the House were abandoned) but it will be too late for our cricket… Maybe it is already too late…

And it will be too late for any government that depends on and gets addicted to the Pirate's golden carrots… Maybe its too late there too…

THE FINAGLING PIRATE

November, 2006

I have waited thirty days before responding to the recent award that was bought and sold to one of Caribbean's most dangerous pirates.

I had to wait to respond reasonably... (not that my tone here is reasonable). I was in shock that our leaders... **our** leaders - some of them trusted, some of them even beloved... some of them to whom we now look for a new direction... That those leaders could make a decision like that. Or that they would keep something like that secret. Or that they would allow such a decision to go forward... fully well knowing how most Antiguans and Barbudan's would react.

They demonstrated no less than contempt for the people... knowing that the deed when done... would be done... their hands soiled... and some of their pockets well oiled... Or, if not those things… they deed was done with a promise of at least - a little pirate grease.

The unforgivable and damning sin of it all is that the reward was transacted by Antigua and Barbuda. It would have been bad enough if the pirate had finagled it from some other bribery responsive, small island Caribbean nation.

But, no... it came from Antigua and Barbuda. Our weak knee'd, beggie-beggie, kow-towing leaders, felt that they had to place a copper sword across that pirate's shoulders.

Remember this... pirates don't want copper... they want gold.
And when you see them accept copper... there is gold hidden
somewhere, not far off... hidden in the mangrove or buried in
our beautiful white sands!

No wonder one of the other really deserving award recipients
of international acclaim is purported to have felt that his/
her moment 'in the sun' was cheapened by this disgraceful
demonstration of brown-nosing by the hat-in-hand, under-the-
table, submissive 'decision-makers'.

And can you imagine the nerve of this pirate that he would
say that those of us who objected to his brazen finagling of the
award... that we objected because of 'envy or jealousy.' Envy
and jealousy of what? Pirate booty? Fools' gold?

All that remains is for us to find out in the next few months,
who gets grease, how much grease they will get, and what they
will use the grease to do.

Of this I am certain... whatever they thought they would get
from this... they won't. That grease will never turn to butter.
Mark my words: Nothing good will come of it! Not for them!
Not for us!

What really bothers me is not so much that the pirate is after
our birthright... Thieves and pirates are always out to pilfer,
filch or 'finagle' your property away from you. What bothers
me is that our week-knee'd leaders have thrown their arms
wide-open to allow the pilfering and filching of what is not
theirs to give.

And yes... it is from Antigua & Barbuda that he wheedled and
wangled the award. But, it seems as though, this pirate has
'captured' the minds of much of the rest of the Caribbean.

He certainly has wheedled his way and inextricably entwined himself into West Indies Cricket… And our Cricketing greats… just like our week-knee'd politicians… have opened their arms – and their pockets – to his wheeling, dealing and manipulating!

Let me emphasize this prediction of the wheedling, wangling and finagling… "Nothing good will come of it!"

And forever more… that award has been tainted and tarnished.

VIOLENCE & DRUG PREVENTION TRAINING NEEDED!

November, 2006

Political, social and economic leaders in Antigua and Barbuda need to come together and initiate powerful strategies to curb the apparently growing levels of violence and drug use among our youth. Despite the best efforts of our youth workers, educators, community officers, law enforcement personnel and other adults who work with youth they have not been able to stem what seems to be a growing problem of violence and drug use among our youth.

Despite the billions of dollars dumped in the "war-on-drugs" by countries around the world, the number of young people using alcohol, tobacco and other drugs has not decreased. And, despite the huge amount of other dollars spent on placing metal detectors in schools, incarcerating young violent offenders, and placing more police officers on the streets and even in some schools, violence among young people has not decreased... it is on the increase. Billions of dollars have also been used to fund the *revolving door* of drug addiction and treatment, building prisons, increasing the number of law enforcement officers, adding magistrates, judges, probation and parole officers, and prisoner officers. All of these things have been tried without much success – other than filling prisons with younger and younger people.

Few people would argue that **a major shift in strategy is needed.**

That shift must go in the *direction of prevention*.

The major assumption of prevention is that if young people are taught key cognitive, behavioral and social skills and presented with critical information, they will be less likely to be involved in delinquent behaviors – including violent behavior and drug use or abuse. Additionally, prevention efforts seek to address and reduce individual, family and community factors that predispose young people to adopt negative lifestyles and behaviors. Prevention programs also enhance and strengthen key protective/resiliency factors that propel youth towards socially acceptable and personally rewarding lifestyles.

In Antigua and Barbuda, there is growing concern about the apparent increase in drug use by youth and their involvement in criminal and violent activities. Political, community and business leaders have recognized that these developments pose a serious social, economic and public health threat. They have also realized that not only does violent activities and drug use and abuse pose an immediate danger to the society, but they also menace the future development of the country's human resources – its youth. Our leaders should therefore be committed to finding solutions to this critical and growing problem.

One solution to the threat of youth violence and drug use and abuse is to train adults and youths in **drug and violence prevention**. Such training would involve all stakeholders from public and private sectors and the community. Participants would include Youth Leaders, Teachers, Prevention Professionals, Community Outreach Officers, Health Professionals, Parole & Probation Officers, Social Workers, Sport Coaches, Psychologists, School Counselors, Addiction Counselors, Youth Workers, Program Supervisors and Managers, Policy Officials, Training Officers, School Administrators and Law Enforcement Officers.

A drug and violence prevention training program would train participants to work with youth to reduce drug use and violence and encourage them to adopt more socially acceptable and life enhancing values and behaviors. On completion of such training, participants would be prepared, certified and qualified to design, develop and implement prevention and intervention activities targeted to pre-teens, teenagers and young adults in Antigua and Barbuda.

Another feature of a national focus on prevention would involve political, social and business leaders in discussions on how they can craft policy measures that would support the shift towards prevention. Political leaders would need to demonstrate their commitment by supporting youth and community workers, and educators with the staff and material resources. Business leaders could support prevention programs by sponsoring prevention community and school activities. Businesses could also sponsor nation-wide prevention initiatives such as radio and television ads focused on youth. Social leaders could add drug and violence prevention programming to their agenda and could serve as and provide volunteers for nationwide prevention events.

The core of all of the above ideas is centered around a comprehensive training strategy where all stakeholders (including political and business leaders) receive a minimum level of training in the scientific methodology of violence and drug prevention.

Plant Seeds!

What kinds of seeds are you sowing in the fields of your mind?

'The kingdom of heaven is like a grain of mustard seed which a man took and sowed in his field; it is the smallest of all seeds, but when it has grown it is the greatest of shrubs and becomes a tree, so that the birds of the air come and make nests in its branches.' (Matthew, 13:31-32).

All of us sow seeds.

If you are in the garden or backyard, you can sow seeds of thorny shrubs, poisonous plants, or trees that bear life-sustaining fruits. However, some of our most important seeds are sown in the fields of our mind. When you ask questions they become like seeds. They will blossom and bear fruit. Depending on your questions, the fruits can be bitter or sweet. I believe that many of our problems occur when we sow the wrong seeds and ask the wrong questions of life. For example, we too often ask 'why' questions when we ought be asking 'how' questions. "How can I get out of this financial mess?" Rather than, "Why me?"

Plant seeds which will grow ideas, strategies, possibilities, and solutions to empower your life.

According to Dottie Walters, "Anyone can cut an apple open and count the number of seeds. But, who can look at a single seed and count the trees and apples? We cannot imagine that this small object is even alive. Yet when it is placed in the soil, a transformation process is started – one that gradually – in time, will nurture and give sustenance to humans, birds and insects.

The smallest question is also like a seed. When it is put in the fertile soil of your mind it contributes to your "tree" of knowledge – which will then produce many "fruits". Yet when we look at the question (like the seed), we cannot see its mighty potential – a potential which lies hidden from casual observation.

Like seeds, your questions will blossom larger than life in the fields of your mind and in the acres of your life.

Caution: Be careful that you not sowing seeds of thorn trees, poisonous plants or parasitic vines *in your mind*! Ensure that you are sowing seeds of empowerment, creative, positive possibilities and success.

By asking the right questions in the right ways, you will be transformed beyond anything currently visible or even imaginable.

"YOUNG PEOPLE" AND CRIME!

November, 2006

In his **2006 Independence** address to the nation, **Prime Minister the Honorable Baldwin Spencer** outlined the various pre-election pledges that his government had already fulfilled only two and a half years into their tenure. The Prime Minister also highlighted a number of the challenges which they and the nation face. One of the challenges he highlighted was the concern his Government has on "the issue of crime and violence in our nation especially the recent upsurge among our young people."

It is undeniable that there seems to have been waves of violence that have shocked many of us to our very core. This is not the Antigua and Barbuda that we know. However, there are several concerns that I would like to raise on the issue of the increase in violence.

Some of the acts of violence perpetrated on our citizens receive huge amounts of publicity. These include break-ins, robberies, and homicides. However there are other acts of violence that are as rampant that do not receive such high levels of publicity. And indeed these other acts of violence do not get high levels of *public outrage*. These include rapes... particularly against children, and family violence that does not include murder.

As a matter of fact, when some of these crimes are committed, there seems to be as much sentiment blaming victims and providing some measure of sympathy for abusers.

I am not sure that the Prime Minister's comments about "crime and violence" in the nation did justice to the crimes against children and violence within families. As a matter of interest, his focus on the "upsurge of violence... among our young people" at the very least, might lead some to believe that a major amount of crimes are committed by youth. While I cannot scientifically challenge that assertion, I can also say that no one has supported it with facts and figures.

In addition, while some youth experts identify "young people" broadly -from birth to 35 years of age, when the general public hears 'youth' or 'young people' they most often think of teenagers or those in their early twenties. (Of course, it also depends on how old you are... My 92 year old mother thinks that I am among the 'young people'!)

Here is my point: We need to be very specific in identifying what the problems are, who are at risk to become victims, who are at risk to become perpetrators, and who are already perpetrators.

The Prime Minister went on to say that his Government believes that "our young people are this nation's future; they must be physically and mentally prepared for it, in addition to possessing the right values to govern and make sound decisions."

In the above statement, Mr. Spencer is not talking about a 35 year old "youth". I would argue that he is not even speaking about a 25 year old "youth"! He is assuredly speaking about 13 year olds and 17 years olds... that is my good guess.

How much violence are those "youths" carrying out? Yes, yes... we certainly have incidents of some violence and criminal behavior by some young people in those age ranges - probably more at an even higher age range like 19... And yes... there might even be some budding gang behavior (apparently fostered and encouraged by a few misguided political comrades).... but the vast majority of our 'young people' are not involved in "crime and violence".

Do we have a problem among those youths? We certainly do. How do we address that problem? See my previous article on "Prevention" for a comprehensive suggestion. I agree with the Prime Minister that we must come together and design and develop creative solutions. And we need to do so now!

However, we have another problem. The problem of violent and criminal acts carried out **by adults** on other adults and on children!

We also need to find specific solutions to deal with the increase of adult criminals sneaking around our premises. We need to find solutions for the increased number of illegal guns that are owned by otherwise law abiding Antiguans and Barbudans. There are several cases of adult violence where individuals shot other adults over emotional and heated conflicts.

In conclusion, I agree that we seem to have increasing levels of violence among youth. We must address that. But we must also address the high levels of criminal and violent behavior perpetrated by adults.

Do You Have "An Attitude of Gratitude"?

November, 2006

"I am thankful to God for each story, each idea, each word... each day!" **Isaac Bashevis**

As I reflect on my personal journey of growth and development, I am ever mindful that I owe much to others. I stand on the shoulders of family members, teachers, friends, acquaintances, and complete strangers. Small gifts of kindness, advice or support at critical times helped to keep me journeying onwards. Such gifts are still powering the winds that help to keep me uplifted each and every day.

As I reflect on these small gifts – I know in my heart – that today would have been totally different without those gifts of yesterday, and tomorrow will be positively different from today: A tit-bit of advice that put me in sync with my internal desire to be a teacher; A one sentence comment that reframed worry into positive wonder and curiosity to take up my spiritual journey; A small envelope with less than $100 that – at the time – was a fortune because it came at the right time. That small gift was the 'tipping' point that helped me decide that I should "go for it", "take the plunge", leave home and attend college.

G. B. Stern says that, *"Silent gratitude is not much help to anyone."* And, so I have been on a mission of finding all of my benefactors and thanking them for their help. Many have responded to me that they didn't know and wasn't aware of the impact of their assistance <u>on</u> me. Truth be told – I am only now coming to the fullest awareness of that myself.

And, it feels good to be sharing this with them.

What about you? Are you harboring "silent gratitude" in your heart?

According to **Shakespeare**, *"Ingratitude is monstrous."* Several of my benefactors are persons whom I can very easily find great fault with – either for things in their public or private lives, or things they have said or done. And, sometimes I do critique them – directly and in person. Yet, I am always grateful – always publicly articulating and demonstrating my deepest appreciation for their support when I needed it. Though it might have been long in the past... theirs was a supportive and unhesitatingly given shoulder shared in the right place and at the right time.

- **How are you demonstrating your gratitude for small acts of kindness?**

- **What are you doing to help others in need?**

- **And, most importantly, what opportunities have you passed up to say, "Thank you" for a benevolent act?**

Whether it happened yesterday or ten years ago, reach out with an attitude of gratitude.

"I am thankful for small mercies. I compared notes with one of my friends who expect everything of the universe, and is disappointed when anything is less than best." **Ralph Waldo Emerson**

In Case of Rain

November, 2006

Recent events in my life have served to re-emphasize to me the importance of constantly ***demonstrating*** faith and belief. I want to emphasize the action word *'demonstrating'*.

There have been many occasions when I have sought divine intervention, many instances when I have asked for celestial inspiration, and countless times when I have just plain prayed for help and assistance.

And in many of those instances when my prayers were answered I was caught unprepared and ***unready*** to take advantage of the very help that I had sought.

If this seems a somewhat philosophical, I hope the following story sheds some light and has the same effect on you that it had on me.

The fields were parched and brown from lack of rain, and the crops lay wilting from thirst. People were anxious and irritable as they searched the sky for any sign of relief. Days turned into arid weeks. No rain came.

The ministers of the local churches called for an hour of prayer on the town square the following Saturday. They requested that everyone bring an object of faith for inspiration.

At high noon on the appointed Saturday the townspeople turned out en masse, filling the square with anxious faces and hopeful hearts. The ministers were touched to see the variety of objects clutched in prayerful hands ... holy books, crosses, prayer beads and various other symbols of religious faith.

When the hour ended, as if on magical command, a soft rain began to fall steadily. Cheers swept the crowd as they held their treasured objects high in gratitude and praise. From the middle of the crowd one faith symbol seemed to overshadow all the others.

A small nine-year old child had brought an umbrella.

Are you ready for what may happen when your prayers are answered and divine intervention brings opportunity knocking at your door steps? For example, if you are seeking to be interviewed for that job of a lifetime, have you dusted off your resume, brushed up on the new jargon in your field, read the latest books and developed some new skills? Have you talked to other experts in the field and gained insights into what's new and what's old? And, have you practiced formulating answers to the tough questions that will likely be asked at your interview?

Are you ready for rain?

CAN YOU IMAGINE?

Wednesday, February 28, 2007

Can you imagine that man called our Prime Minister a liar?

Can you imagine that man said that our Prime Minister is an inept leader?

Can you imagine that man called our Prime Minister deceitful?

Can YOU imagine that man called OUR Prime Minister misguided?

Can YOU imagine that man called YOUR Prime Minister un-statesmanlike?

Can you imagine that this same man, after having called our Prime Minister a liar, a misguided, deceitful, un-statesmanlike and an inept leader that he is appealing to Antiguans and Barbudans to be on his side?

Can YOU imagine?

I can imagine. Yep. I can!

Not only did he insult OUR Prime Minister... but in so doing he insulted both YOU and I... His very demeanor has been an insult to us. His very presence in this country is an insult to us. His every action has been to insult us. He has insulted us with every word he utters. His every position is a calculated insult to us.

There are thousands of us in Antigua and Barbuda, and thousands of us around the world who have been warning that the same man has ulterior motives... that his intentions are not good... at least not for us... and not even for those Judas Antiguans he pays a couple pieces of his tarnished silver coins to do his dirty work for him. Shame on him... and shame on all those around him. And shame on all those who speak for him... and defend him. Shame on those well paid Judas Antiguans!

I hasten to add that some of the people who slave for him are just ordinary workers... ordinary Antiguans who found work in his company. For many of them their public responses are different from their private responses. In one word... they dislike him intensely... but they love his money. Of course... the higher their positions the more they have to display their loyalty... But our criticisms are not targeted at them.

Our criticisms are targeted at the local overseers and those over-sea-ers!

Anyway... Finally, the Honourable, W. Baldwin Spencer, Prime Minister of Antigua and Barbuda, an honest, sensitive and sensible, peaceful and peace-loving, concerned and committed, born and bred, roots man Antiguan... has awakened... has put on his armor, and is 'stiffening his sinews'! He now has the 'look in his eye' and the fierceness in his spirit. This is the man who said to Antiguans and Barbudans: "We got them! We got them!"

And Now he can say... "We got **him**! No let he go - We got **him**!"

And there are those of us who say... "At last! At last! Finally!"

There were signs of it coming since his Xmas speech when he demoted the turncoat investor... who now has gone back to showing his real colors – red of course! He never left... only pretended and undermined the whole UPP machinery. Even destroying the good relationship... the almost life long relationship... the brothers-in-arms relationship... between the Deputy and the Leader! But now... he is gone! At least, I hope so!

And so too – is that unhealthy alliance with that man, that pirate who insulted OUR Prime Minister... and who insulted both YOU and I. I hope he gone too... but just maybe... Them say money longer than rope... Or is it time... well both... Money and time longer than rope... And he got both.

Ho, Ho, Ho!

Friday, March 09, 2007

Recent headlines across the Caribbean state "**LIAT To Buy C-Star!**" Other headlines also indicate that C-Star will "*Lend shareholder governments US$55 million*" to buy C-Star and pay their debts!

Huh? C-Star will lend **LIAT** money to buy C-Star *from* C-Star???

According to one newspaper, this was said by Dr. Ralph Gonsalves, Prime Minister of St. Vincent & the Grenadines, who apparently is the spokesman for the LIAT shareholder governments. Gonsalves also reportedly said, "We are buying Caribbean Star... the question is whether we buy the assets or we buy the whole airline!"

I was floored... once again. Knocked down! I couldn't believe it. Once again our leaders have allowed themselves to be swindled by THE modern day pirate of the Caribbean. In broad daylight. Conned not only right in front of the faces... but by their own willing agreement!

Something else is going on. It can't be just stupidity!

Let's look at this a little more closely. Now... let me be clear... I am not trying to be an **analyst**! I am just simply trying to understand this issue.

- C-Star was founded to compete with LIAT.

- C-Star competed aggressively with LIAT and by all accounts C-Star purposely and successfully undermined LIAT's profitability by establishing predatory pricing practices!

- From the very beginning, it was obvious that C-Star's leadership's primary goal was to fatally wound LIAT and bring it down. All of this so that C-Star would then become the choice airline of the islands and in the process... it would swallow LIAT!

- That did not happen!

- Yes LIAT was wounded. But in the process C-Star was losing money in gushes.

And so, C-Star's leadership seems to have revised its plan...

What was the new plan? Well, they needed to stop the millions of dollars that was gushing down the C-Star toilet. So... why not sell C-Star to LIAT?

Hey... not only will "I" stop my money from gushing into the toilet... but I will get back some of the money that I lost. Unhuh --- But they won't have the money to buy C-Star... so if I lend them the money to buy C-Star and pay off some of their debts, I will get more of my money back from the interest on the loan. **Ho, Ho Ho and a bottle of ~~Cavalier~~ Courvoisier Cognac!**

Yep... And, if those leaders are as foolish as they have been, as part of the deal... not only will I "sell" C-Star to them — not only will I lend them the money so that they can buy my failed C-Star from me – But maybe I will also get them to give me 35% of **LIAT** in the process! **Ho Ho Ho and a bottle of** ~~Sunset Rum~~ **Johnny Walker!**

What a plan!

1. I sell C-Star to LIAT! I unload the failed C-Star on those governments! Now *their* money will be gushing down the toilet!

2. I lend them the money to buy C-Star from **me** to pay off some of their debts. So now they owe me... and I will continue to reap the benefits from the interest for years and years...

3. I also get to own 35% of LIAT! As a result I become the single majority shareholder!!! *Ho, Ho, Ho*!

4. *Plus*, they will come back to beg me more money... Most airlines all over the world are failing... LIAT will not make it - not without me and my great leadership (even though I couldn't make C-Star successful). So when they borrow more money from me... I will increase my shares... until I own most of it...! In addition, I will not only get more land in Antigua... I will get land in St. Vincent too... I don't think I can fool those Bajans... but why not try? I got those Bajan cricketing greats... so maybe I can get the politicians... too. Although that Mia Mottley (notice the last name)... seems to be different!

5. So, this will enhance my ability to execute my **master plan**... (more on this in another BLOG) **HO, Ho, Ho and a bottle of** ~~Mount Gay~~ **Chardonnay.**

Explain "Why" to me!

So, can someone explain to me why our illustrious government leaders have agreed to this nefarious plan?

Maybe it is I who don't understand! Maybe it is because I am not an economist… or maybe I am slow… or worse… daft!

But something else is going on… this cannot be just plain stupidity. As one of those leaders said several months ago… "When we explain it… everyone will understand."

Well, I need to hear that explanation because right now, it seems to me our leaders are not only willing… but enthusiastic victims of the buccaneering exploits of the #1 pirate of the Caribbean!

NEW SIDEWALKS!

Saturday, March 31, 2007

My 92 year-old mother is singing the praises of the UPP
government. Why? Because when she goes to shop in St. Johns,
she can walk along the sidewalks without fear of being hit
by a car. She likes the wider, flatter and lower sidewalks. The
only things she says that she has to look out for are those red
painted, poorly designed grates. She says that the bars should
be placed closer together. But, she is not really complaining.

So... she is thankful and surprised.

Why surprised? Well... the sidewalks and the road
improvements were not there the last time she walked through
the city. She is amazed at the speed with which the project is
being completed. She is further amazed, because in Antigua, it
is highly unusual for projects... particularly public projects...
especially public projects conducted by Public Works... to be
done quickly. And when you add... efficiently, effectively and
attractively... well that is historically unheard of.

Now she knows that Public Works had help. She knows that
the Cubans seemed to have put us to shame and that that
might have provided the necessary prick on our pride to spur
our Public Works' staff to respond positively to the challenge.
And respond they have... and well... so far... so good.

But the stronger prick and push came not from the Cubans
but from the imminent arrival of Cricket World Cup. For
months... maybe longer... just about everyone in the country

has been fussing about the need to fix the roads... all roads. Even some Ministers of the current Government seemed to have been discontented with the situation. There were charges from some elected officials that the Ministry of Finance was not releasing the money for public projects. There were counter charges that Public Works was not providing the proper documentation to request the necessary funds.

But all of the squabbling dissipated when everyone realized that the opening date for CWC was just around the corner! There was a deadline. There was no getting around it. There was no getting away from it. The date was set in stone. So the stones had to be worked. And so, what needed to be done was done – quickly. And the city is being transformed.

So it took the imminent arrival of CWC to drive our Government to implement this project of upgrading the city. According to local DJ and radio personality Serpent, it seems as though we need to bring CWC here to Antigua every month in order for Government to complete all of the projects that it has promised.

Sad... but true.

So... what other events might we the people highlight that would get a similar response from the Government? How can we get the Government to fix all the roads and alleys? How can we influence them, or push them to really make significant adjustments to the airport? What can we do to get them to implement serious programming to address the apparently high levels of crime and violence? What kind of pricking is needed to have them foster deep and lasting improvements to our education system?

And what do we have to do to get any Government… UPP or whoever… to continuously deliver on the projects that they promise?

Elections? Maybe we should have some kind of election every two years. I think that we need to change from an appointed Senate to an elected one. Then we need to change elections for the Lower House from every five years to every four years. The Senate would also be elected every four years. Both elections would be held two years apart. So, for example, the next election for the Lower House would be held in 2008 (and every four years thereafter), and the elections for our new Senate would be held in 2010 (and every four years thereafter.

That would keep politicians hopping. That would keep them delivering. And, we the people would see a never ending stream of projects – creatively, efficiently, effectively and attractively done – just like the sidewalks in St. Johns.

By the way… why were the grates painted **red**?

THEY CHASED US AWAY

Sunday, April 01, 2007

What has happened in Antigua and the rest of the Caribbean during the current Cricket World Cup showcase has a huge significance for us.

The most critical issue of course is the draconian, colonialistic restrictions that CWC organizers placed on the islands hosting the matches.

The very nature of the restrictions placed on us by CWC organizers reminds me of what I have read of our colonial history. CWC came to our shores... used our facilities... had us spend millions of dollars of infrastructural development and then restricted us from putting our stamp on the games. They restricted us from marketing our local products. They restricted our local companies from marketing their services. They restricted our people from behaving and acting like Antiguans, Barbudans, Guyanese, Trinidadians, Barbadians, Jamaicans, Kittitians, Grenadians, Dominicans, St. Lucians... They restricted us from being who we are.

And we allowed them. We kowtowed to them. We said, "Yes Masah!" "Anything you say, Masah!" "You get anything you want, Masah." "You want anything else, Sah?"

Veteran cricket writer Tony Becca says it is the International Cricket Council (ICC) that is responsible for the poor involvement of the local people in the showpiece event. "They (the ICC and organizers) want tourists from other parts of the

World to come but ignored the local populations" Becca said. He also said, "I have covered many World Cups and what I saw (in the past) was that the majority of the crowd has been local." He continued, "The ICC thought the World Cup as a golden goose and chased the local people out assuming that large numbers would come from abroad and they would not need local support."

And so, they chased us away.

One hundred US dollars for a ticket! That is $270 Eastern Caribbean Dollars. In a region where many people don't even earn that in a week... the CWC organizers were really catering to the rich, the elite business class and to the so-called tourists.

So, they chased us away.

And the seats which were available to the local populations were limited. Very limited. At least... they were limited until the last moment when CWC realized that their thousands and thousands of tourists just weren't coming.

And they lied about the numbers.

At first we heard that 50,000 'tourists' were coming to Antigua. We were going to have to get cruise ships to accommodate all those tourists since we did not have enough rooms and beds here. Entrepreneurs were encouraged to invest in bed and breakfast accommodations and build motels. Ordinary citizens were encouraged to spruce up empty rooms in their houses to accommodate the thousands of CWC 'tourists' who would need a room for a few nights! Then the figures were downgraded... to 30,000... to 20,000... to 15,000... to... well... who knows what the final figures will be?

Now we weren't talking about Barbadians, Jamaicans, Guyanese and Trinidadians coming here. And they certainly weren't talking about Antiguans and Barbudans returning home for the matches… nope. ICC/CWC didn't care about them… and didn't factor them in.

And of course, they didn't care about those here at home either.

So they didn't factor us in. Instead, they chased us away.

Why did they do that? They certainly didn't expect the Caribbean masses to buy those US$100 tickets! They expected the seats to be filled with Australians, New Zealanders, British… and with a scattering of Indian, Pakistani and Sri Lankan supporters.

Racism?

Or were they making sure that the West Indies Team would not have the massive numbers of supporters who would form a powerful 12th man?

Now there are other ways they made sure that even those of us who were foolish enough to want to buy those costly tickets could not get them. I stood in a line of 60 persons at their one purchasing site in St. Johns for one hour. In that one hour, they processed five persons!!! I left my son in the line, went home, got online, purchased the tickets, went back to the purchasing office, waved my receipt in the face of the security guard, walked inside and picked up my tickets. My son was still in line – facing a four to five hour wait!

They chased us away and I should have stayed away. But… I wanted the exposure for my sons… That's a limp argument… because… well…

They chased us away.

Of course, I guess ICC/CWC had a colonial view of us. They probably didn't expect locals to be 'sophisticated' enough to purchase their tickets online. Almost all the people who were in the expedited line with online receipts were Aussies or Brits!

Yep, they intended to chase us away. It worked... because we have stayed away.

Why? Because we clearly understand... this is not our 'ting'. This is their thing. So they can have it...

There are other issues of course. Like the wimpish, spineless negotiators who represented us. Like the spinning that is being done by our local officials about how we will benefit in the future as a result of spending over $300 million. Like the financial impact on tourism during this period that stems from those stupid visa requirements... Like the fact that it took the advent of CWC to push our government to fix sidewalks and some roads...

But those issues are for another day.

Today, they chased us away.

So, tomorrow and the next day... and the next day... we will stay away.

THE RISING VIOLENCE

Friday, April 27, 2007

The Rising Violence: *Let's Take Action* - **Now!**

There is a growing sense of helplessness among Antiguans as we hear and read about the increasing acts of violence - particularly gun violence - that seems to be spinning out of control.

There might have been a time when some people felt that they were safe from the robberies and hold ups that were once the primary acts of violence. Now, everyone realizes that he or she is at risk. We realize that our children are at risk. And we realize that our elderly are at risk.

This is serious.

What is even more serious... and frightening, is the apparent inability of our law enforcement to catch the perpetrators of these violent acts. I am not even talking about preventing the violence... I am referencing 'catching the criminals'. The fact that our law enforcement... who has been agitating for higher salaries... can't catch these criminals means that we are all at risk for the criminals to continue their rampage of violence, thefts, break-ins and other acts of lawlessness.

As an aside... or maybe this is central to the whole issue... is the fact that our law enforcement officers don't seem to understand that there is a correlation between performance, productivity, results... ---- and pay raise!

The Government needs to take immediate and strong action. Now. There is no bigger crisis existing in our nation today than the threat that the violence poses to all of us. It threatens our economy. It threatens our daily lives. It threatens us while we sleep. It threatens our feelings of being safe. It threatens us as we go to work. It threatens us as we go home from work. It threatens us on the bus and in our cars. It threatens us in our homes... our supposedly safe havens. It threatens our children at school and at play.

The Government needs to demand action from the police... and if we don't get results - we need to replace the police leadership with highly trained, highly skilled, results oriented, proven law enforcement leaders from where-ever we can get them. Now for me that is a stretch - since I am adamantly opposed to bringing foreign nationals to our shores and putting them in leadership positions. But we are in a crisis... and so we need to contract the kind of police leadership that presents a modern, sophisticated, technological approach to getting the results that we need. And then we need to give our own young and upcoming police world class training. When we get that new leadership we then need to make available to them the sophisticated forensic and investigative instruments and technology that they need to get the job done.

The Government also needs to begin a comprehensive multi-dimensional violence prevention campaign. This campaign should have several facets:

1. Violence prevention targeted to adults and involve public education in conflict resolution & negotiation and anger management.

2. Mechanisms available to the public that include mediation services and conflict resolution services. Some of these should be availed through the courts whereby

individuals might be 'sentenced' to attend anger management or conflict resolutions classes.

3. Violence prevention targeted to young adults and teenagers who are out of school. This would involve education in some of the above subjects. However, two key areas of focus would be job skills training and drug prevention education.

4. Violence prevention and drug education activities at all schools and at all grade levels. The focal points of these school-based trainings would be: Life skills (effective communication, conflict resolution, self-esteem building, study skills for academic success, how to deal with negative peer pressure and bullying, etc.), values education and character building educational programming.

5. An integrated and comprehensive island-wide network of after-school activities involving academics (home-work help, remedial work, etc), guided sports activities (with a values education component), performing arts (plays, dance, etc), computer & technology, and art.

6. Treatment programs for drug addiction and alcoholism. The Government needs to contract with qualified counseling professionals to provide confidential and ongoing treatment services to addicts and alcoholics. Such services should be provided at every clinic.

7. Rehabilitation Services for Juvenile Offenders. This is seen by well placed officials as a critical need. Such services would include some of those mentioned above.

8. A Probation and Parole Office should be developed to monitor and track the activities of criminal offenders.

This office should also oversee the provision of re-entry programs for offenders who are re-entering society. These services would entail job training, mental health services and substance abuse services.

I could go on. But I think that you get the picture. The Government has to develop and implement NOW a comprehensive and integrated program to deal with this menace to society. Failure to *adequately* address the crisis of violence in our society will lead to such deterioration that it will negatively impact the bright future of our twin island state.

Giving Up Too Soon!

Wednesday, February 28, 2007

Have there been times in your life when you felt like you wanted to give up – thinking that you had tried everything – exhausted your energy, your resources, or even your patience? You may have even postponed, or put on the back burner, projects that you did not quite achieve in the time allotted or to the degree of success that you had desired.

No… I am not talking about dreams and goals that you have had, or unfulfilled New Year resolutions. I am speaking about projects and tasks that you had actually started.

I had always wanted to publish a book. No… not write… publish. You see, I had already written several books over the years, but could not get over the hurdle of getting someone – anyone – to publish any of my books.

Yet, I had met several authors, most of whom had the same story… They spent years writing their book. Then, they spent several frustrating years trying to find a publisher. Yep. That was my story.

But their story had a different ending. They found a publisher. How? Everyone had a different solution for finding a publisher. Yet, they all shared one thing in common… perseverance. They never gave up.

Such perseverance is particularly common among famous and very successful authors:

- Louis L'Amour, successful author of more than 100 western novels with more than 200 million copies in print, received more than 350 rejections before he found a publisher.

- British writer John Creasy received 774 rejections before he was able to publish his first story. He went on to write 564 books – using 14 different names.

- Dr. Seuss' first children's book, *And to Think That I Saw It on Mulberry Street,* was rejected by 27 publishers. The twenty-eighth publisher Vanguard Press sold 6 million copies of the book. All of his books went on to sell a total of more than 100 million copies.

- The first *Chicken Soup for the Soul* was rejected by 123 (33 in New York, and 90 in Anaheim) publishers. Eight million copies of that book has since been sold, and 53 million copies (and counting) of the thirty-three title series have been sold world wide.

- Early in his career, Alex Haley, author of Roots, received one rejection letter every week for four years.

One of the authors whom I interviewed on the way to my first published book, **Ask, Seek, Knock** - shared the following story with me. I hope that it will inspire you or someone to whom you will have passed this newsletter to.

> A man meets a guru in the road. The man asks the guru, "Which way is success?"
>
> The bearded sage does not speak, but points to a place off in the distance.

The man, thrilled by the prospect of quick
and easy success, rushes off in the appropriate
direction. Suddenly, there comes a loud "splat."

Eventually, the man limps back, tattered and
stunned, assuming he must have misinterpreted
the message. He repeats his question to the guru,
who again points silently in the same direction.

The man obediently walks off once more. This
time the splat is deafening, and when the man
crawls back, he is bloody, broken, tattered, and
irate. "I asked you which way is success," he
screams at the guru. "I followed the direction you
indicated. And all I got was splatted! No more of
this pointing! Talk!"

Only then does the guru speak, and what he says
is this: "Success is that way. Just a little past
splat."

Whether your project involves writing, building your career,
or improving your performance and productivity… success lies
just beyond the point at which you felt like giving up… or
just beyond the place where you fell down… or just beyond the
next bend in the road…. Just a little past splat!

Success is that way. Keep going.

View Change as Challenge!

Friday, March 02, 2007

Are you experiencing troubling or difficult changes on your job, at home, in your social life or in your community?

Do you see these changes as tragedies, trials or tribulations? Or do you see them as calamities, catastrophes, or unnecessary complications?

What is your response to these changes in your life or circumstances? Are you reacting in anger, fear or hostility? Or are you only irritated, frustrated, or mildly upset? Are you stressed out and threatened by the changes which you are anticipating or those which have already occurred?

In one of my keynotes on how to successfully deal with change: Change Your Life & Keep The Changes You Desire – One critically important strategy that I share is that we should **"View Change as Challenge!"**

Here are a few steps on how to do reframe "Change" into "Challenge"

First, remember this too shall pass. Think clearly about what this means. I regularly tell myself that "It is night now. Yes, it is dark. Yet, morning will come. Light will come." That does not mean that I only wait for the morning. Yes, I will bring my own light to the issue… And, I know – that eventually – things will change. For the better!

Ask yourself... What can I change in myself? What can I do, now, that will allow for me to have a different reaction to this change? What about me can I change or adjust so that I can empower myself.

Rephrase the "the problem" into a "challenge" and then into a positive opportunity.

"There is in the worst of fortunes the best of chances for a happy change." Euripides.

"Some men see things as they are and say 'why?'

I dream things that never were, and say, 'Why not?'" Robert Kennedy

Convert fear, anger and other limiting emotions such as worry, anxiety, despondency, denial or avoidance into positive energy. Energy means action. Action means doing something positive that will help to alleviate your stress and empower you to act purposefully – moving you toward a well-defined goal.

Analyze the situation. What is the problem? Look at solutions....What can you do now? What can you do later? Who can you turn to for assistance? Who has had a similar situation like this? What can you learn from them?

Act calmly and persistently. What ever you do – take decisive and relentless action! Do not stop until you have successfully handled the situation.

Don't stop! Do not stop after you have successfully deal with the challenge! Now you must take action to fortify yourself to prevent this particular issue from becoming a "problem"! This may mean: keeping your resume updated; starting your job search today; establishing a home-based, part time business; building new and more supportive relationships; getting rid of the toxic relationships in your life; starting an exercise program, changing your nutritional habits, and supplementing your diet with vitamins and minerals; Examining your "Globe of Life" and developing a personal vision and mission for specific areas.

Whenever you are faced with "change" you must view it as a "challenge" – an opportunity to do something different that will lead to you having more personal power.

Ask yourself empowering questions. Seek creative solutions. Knock and take decisive and relentless action.

Do You Have High Blood Pressure?

Saturday, March 10, 2007

There are times when we turn a blind eye to the realities of what's happening in our lives. We consciously or unconsciously avoid asking the key questions that we should. We become comfortable with personal and professional conditions that are much less than optimal. As things decline, rather than make small adjustments, we accept the deteriorating situations and do nothing. We allow things to get worse and to move slowly towards disaster until it is almost too late to make a comeback.

This was the case with an executive who I was coaching. He had just turned 50 years old and 'suddenly' realized that his blood pressure was 140/90. Five years ago, his blood pressure was 125/83 and apparently had 'quietly' increased steadily. Over the years, he had resisted exercising and changing his diet. According to him he was 'too busy' and too focused on 'living life' and fulfilling his career dream. He had put on 29 pounds in five years… and those pounds were in the wrong places!

These were subtle, gradual, creeping changes which now, five years later, were still not enough to persuade him to be overly concerned. That is, until I got him to project and track these changes five years into the future. I got him to understand his life backwards and forwards so that he would have a life – today **and** tomorrow.

And so I asked him, "If you continued to do the things that you have done over the **past** five years, and **based on the rate of** *progression* over *that* time period, what might your weight and blood pressure (and health) be five years from now **into the future?**"

Though he was resistant and slow to respond, the answers to that question gradually shook him awake, and he began to look more closely at his past **and current** activities. Those answers jerked him (still somewhat reluctantly) into planning and implementing (minor) lifestyle changes which he could easily and painlessly integrate.

Once we recognize that negative shifts have taken place in our lives, it behooves us to decide how we will respond. Ask yourself: If I continue to do the things that I have been doing, what will life be like in one year? Two years? Five years?

Ask questions. Hear the answers. Take action! Those are the three keys of personal and professional transformation.

Responding to 360 Degree Feedback

March 12, 2007

360 Degree feedback methods help employees receive performance feedback from supervisors, direct reports, peers and in some cases, customers. According to some experts, the most helpful feedback comes from observers who focus on the behaviors and skills of the person seeking the feedback.

The general purpose of the 360 Degree feedback is to help each individual gain insights of how he or she is perceived by others regarding their strengths and weakness. The goal of course is not just to have many different persons rate another person's performance… but for that person to use the information to increase their performance, productivity and overall effectiveness.

For the past several years, I have coached many executives through this process and have seen a variety of responses to the feedback they receive. In a significant number of cases, individuals receiving such feedback have problems handling the difficult and sometimes unflattering responses that are offered by colleagues and others.

I was recently asked by someone who is going through this process to advise them on how to handle this difficulty. In response, I have developed a list of guiding perspectives and suggestions.

Perspectives & Suggestions:

- Do not look at the feedback as criticism. These comments are another person's perceptions about you.

- These are how other people see, hear, smell taste and experience you as you interact with them.

- Do not engage in trying to guess who said what and why they said it.

- You do not have to be defensive. You do not have to explain. Just take it in.

- Do not see the feedback as malicious remarks from people who do not like you.

- Irrespective of their intentions, they have done you a great service. They have told you what you did not know or what you may have avoided knowing or facing.

- They have revealed their inner reactions to your personality, to your communication and to your interactions with them.

- Understand that what one person has revealed... there may be many others who privately agree. Now you know what has been hidden from you.

- They have educated you and opened your eyes. Now **you** must open your ears. *And, you must open your heart.*

- You can never again be in denial with regards to how these persons are impacted by you or how they perceive you. You can never again say that you did not know.

- **The key is this: What will you do with their _gift_ to you?**

- Will you be defensive? Will you draw a line in the sand and say, "I did so and so... because.... I am like this... because you don't really understand me... because you were not really listening to me... because I did not mean so and so... you really misunderstood me... blah blah blah..."

- Or will you say... "Well, I have a lot of work to do – to change how am perceived... to make my intensions more clear."

- "I will communicate more effectively to reduce how I 'rub people the wrong way.'" "I will reduce my abrasiveness..."

- "I will enhance my ability to lead, to motivate, to influence and inspire."

- "I will demonstrate more of my ability to listen and understand others."

- "I will demonstrate that I can take advantage of these insights... this information and that I can change in positive ways."

- "I will not hold onto 'who I thought I was' or 'what I thought I was doing'."

- "I will now set goals in order to change me first."

- "I have the capacity, the ability and desire to change to be better… not bitter; to grow, learn and develop – not defend!"

Those are my thoughts on the attitude that is needed to derive the greatest benefit from critical feedback of others.

MOUNT BARACK OBAMA: WHY NOT?

December 28, 2008

When the Honourable Baldwin Spencer, Prime Minister of Antigua and Barbuda indicated that he would start the process of renaming Boggy Peak to Mount Barack Obama many Antiguans vociferously objected.

I found none of their arguments against the renaming persuasive.

Some said that Barack Obama had done nothing for Antigua and Barbuda and we should wait and see if he does anything during his forthcoming tenure as President of the United States.

Others said that the fact that President Elect Obama was going to be the first African American U.S. President was no reason for Antiguans to be celebrative to the degree that we would elevate his name to such 'heights'. Others contended that though this might be a signal moment for African Americans, it was not an important moment for Antiguans.

Many of those opposed to the renaming of Boggy Peak pointed to our own heroes who they contended we should first give that level of prominence to. Others proposed that we first consider elevating regional historic greats like Bob Marley... rather than raise up a virtually unknown and new to the world stage American politician.

Others argued that to elevate Barack Obama on the basis that he is to be the first U.S. President of African origin, is tantamount to racism and does a disservice to our nation's diverse population. (I have heard this argument before from those who are objecting to the development of heritage tourism in Antigua. They argue that we already have 'heritage tourism' in the form of the Dockyard and the old Betty's Hope sugar mill. These naysayers to heritage tourism contend that to focus on Antigua's slave history and to develop monuments and shrines to 'our' great great grandparents – the former slaves who suffered so greatly at the hands of the monsterous slave owners and their almost sociopathic, lackey overseers – would open wounds that we should leave closed.)

Well... many of those who make this last argument are the grandsons and granddaughters of those slave owners and/ or their overseers. Others who make this argument are, or represent the new colonialists who have come to our shores... literally – our sweet shores (the sugar is now on the beaches). Their argument is not worth responding to... at least not in this article... although I am very tempted to do so!

Of course the foregoing are only some of the arguments presented against the idea of a 'Mount Obama'.

In this article, I only want to draw attention to some of the current names of places in Antigua and ask if the origins of those names mean anything to any Antiguan... well at least to any Afro-Antiguan. Most of the names certainly don't mean anything to me. And many of the names that I do know something about are of individuals I would prefer to not have known about or have to reference each time I think of, or speak of a specific location in my country.

I don't know and don't care who Bolans, Urlings, Bendals, Briggins, Jennings, Swetes, or Ottos were named for. As a matter of discourse, I can guess though… and I can dig into some his-story book to find out. Just as I can guess that Gunthroppes, Burkes Estate, Herberts Estate, Montepelier and Sandersons were probably named after plantation owners. All of whom, in some way or the other - used, abused, raped, violated, murdered and/or committed genocide on their slave populations. Not once… but they did these things as a matter of course… and over a long period of time. And they committed the same vile offences on the offspring of the slaves…

Not all of those persons committing these heinous crimes on slaves would have been slave owners or overseers. A significant number would have been the government administrators, merchants and officials (even of the church) who provided the glue that held the whole system of slavery together.

All of them – slave owners, overseers, merchants, and government and other officials profited and benefitted socially, physically, sexually, financially… and emotionally… from their exploitation of the slaves they claimed to own and the system they represented… A system that was the lifeblood of the British Empire… from St. John's to Bombay and from Perth to Kingston.

As I write this article I realize how annoyed a small few of you – the readers are. Well… it is interesting for you to be annoyed if you see nothing wrong in perpetuating the names of those murderous plantation owners, their vile overseers and the colonial administrators and officials. John Hughes, Gilbert, Willock, Belmont and Glanville are all guilty… and we must decry them – the only way we can – posthumously.

Let's not forget some other names that we know not whence they are from: Clarks (Hill), Gray's (Hill), Willikies, Pares, Seatons, Parham, Yepton, Cades, Barnes (Hill), Fitch(es)

(Creek), Cobbs (Cross), Carlisle (Bay), Patterson, Claremont, Wapping (Lane), and Redcliffe (Street). We know what they stood for... what they perpetuated and what they benefitted from.

Now I know that Pappy Sammy has helped us tremendously in digging in and examining the history of Africans in Antigua and Barbuda. So, with some research, we can probably pin down who most of these "men" were. But, those historical names do not give me any sense of ownership or pride. Quite the opposite, they highlight a sordid chapter in world history as having taken part in or contributed in no small measure to the genocide of Africans in the Caribbean.

Every time that you call one of these names you are giving credence to, showing appreciation for, testifying to, or highlighting the odious significance of these slave owners and their overseers. Each time we call their names we memorialize them. Each time they are mentioned as our addresses, we are unknowingly... and uncaringly... are commemorating their dastardly and sordid crimes against the spirits of our ancestors.

Should we say their names in the same breath as Pappy Sammy, Ernest Williams, Nellie Robinson, V.C. Bird, George Walter, or Tim Hector? I suggest that it is sacrilege to do so.

But we have not given that any thought.

Every chance we get we honor the one-armed, one eyed British naval rogue after whom the dockyard is named. There are many in Antigua who speak that name with deep pride (mostly the great great grandchildren of overseers and British, Scottish and Irish indentured servants). But I do not... And as I understand it, many of those celebrated buildings in Dockyard and certainly the walls around it were built with the sweat and blood forced and beaten out of slaves.

Dockyard... does not and never has been — for me — a place for tribute.

In defending the island from that site... the British celebrated naval rogue was defending a colony of Britain, the plantations of the slave holders and a fountain of income for the royalty in England. He was not defending the slave population — the only consequence to whom would have been to have new slave masters who spoke French.

Then of course there was Drake and Hawkins Streets named after two British privateers. These men were nothing less than state sponsored pirates... terrorists in today's terminology... wreaking havoc on both French and Spanish ships and on the populations of coastal towns in the French Caribbean Islands and coastal Spanish cities in Central and South America. These are not men who we, or anyone, (except for the afore-mentioned descendants of slave owners, overseers and merchants) should celebrate or elevate. We rightly replaced their names with the names of our local heroes.

There is a case to be made that we should have started the process of renaming many of our villages and other sites with names of people who have inspired so many of us: Nelson Mandela, Marcus Garvey, Mahatma Gandhi, Hannibal, Shaka, Pele, Sojourner Truth, Fidel Castro — names that raise a different level of consciousness and give us a unique national flavor.

We already have St. Johns, St. Mary's, St. Paul's, St. Phillip's, St. Luke's, and St. Peter's parishes. Therefore, I am not opposed to recognizing a few other names related to spiritual or religious identities like Buddha and Mohammed whose life and words are and have been an inspiration to so many... here, in this region and around the world. I know that this idea will probably trigger apoplectic type seizures in many of you. But, let's take at least a balanced stance at who we memorialize. We did not have any input in naming our parishes... so why not make some changes there also?

And so here we are at the point of the renaming of the highest point on the island: Mount Barack Obama. And based on the foregoing discussion... it is a good thing.

ABOUT THE AUTHOR

Marcus M. Mottley is a Clinical Psychologist, certified Neuro-Linguistic Programming Practitioner, and certified Hypnotherapy Practitioner. He provides services in Human Capital and Organizational Consulting and Executive Coaching, and operates an online and offline Coaching/Mentoring business providing services to clients worldwide.

He is a certified training manager and a professional speaker who has been a member of Toastmasters International, the American Seminar Leaders Association and the National Speakers Association. He is a three-time winner (2002, 2004 & 2005) of Toastmasters International Public Speaking Contest for District 36 (Washington, DC & Maryland – representing over 160 Toastmasters' Clubs).

Marcus grew up in Tinning Village, Grays Farm, St. Johns, Antigua. He graduated from the St. Joseph's Academy and worked as an airline employee with LIAT, a teacher at the Greenbay Government School, a Family Life Educator with the Ministry of Health, and as a Labour Relations Officer with the Employers' Federation. During this time he played and coached soccer, was involved in Martial Arts and also had his own Hi-Fi business!

While most of these experiences helped to shape and form him, it was his work as teacher and coach that was most transformative. He believes that he learned more from the students than he taught. As a teacher, his childhood love of philosophy and advanced learning was rekindled. It was also at this time that he started writing articles – many of which have been lost in the dust of time while a few have survived and are published in this book.

He recounts that during one morning's motivational session at Greenbay School, he spoke to the students about uplifting their lives and educating themselves way beyond what they thought was possible. He referenced that tired cliché: "Shoot for the moon – If you miss, you'll be among the stars." As he stood before the students, he clearly heard a voice in his head responding: "What about you? Why don't you show them rather than tell them. Be the example! Why don't you shoot for the moon? Show them what's possible. Educate *yourself*!"

From that moment forward, he was on a mission to educate himself. Today, he is still on that mission since he believes that no one is learned… we are all in a state and in a process of continuous *learning*…!

Dr. Mottley is the author of **Ask, Seek, Knock** (2004), **How to Drug & Alcohol Proof Your Child** (eBook – 2006) and co-author of **Get Help For Domestic Violence** (eBook – 2007).

He is available to facilitate meetings and conduct workshops, seminars, keynote addresses, executive coaching and to provide consultations for organizations and individuals. He can be reached at mpowerme@gmail.com or online at one of his websites: www.Speaktrain.com, www.SupportForTrainers.com, www.SpeakAndTrain.com, www.Prevent-Drug-Abuse.com, www.HelpForDomesticViolence.com.